SQUADRO

No. 33

THE BREWSTER
BUFFALO

PHIL H. LISTEMANN

ISBN: 979-1096490-40-0

Copyright

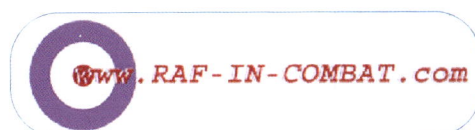

Colour profiles: Gaetan Marie/Bravo Bravo Aviation

GLOSSARY OF TERMS

PERSONEL :

(AUS)/RAF: Australian serving in the RAF
(BEL)/RAF: Belgian serving in the RAF
(CAN)/RAF: Canadian serving in the RAF
(CZ)/RAF: Czechoslovak serving in the RAF
(NFL)/RAF: Newfoundlander serving in the RAF
(NL)/RAF: Dutch serving in the RAF
(NZ)/RAF: New Zealander serving in the RAF
(POL)/RAF: Pole serving in the RAF
(RHO)/RAF: Rhodesian serving in the RAF
(SA)/RAF: South African serving in the RAF
(US)/RAF - RCAF : American serving in the RAF or RCAF

RANKS

G/C : Group Captain
W/C : Wing Commander
S/L : Squadron Leader
F/L : Flight Lieutenant
F/O : Flying Officer
P/O : Pilot Officer
W/O : Warrant Officer
F/Sgt : Flight Sergeant
Sgt : Sergeant
Cpl : Corporal
LAC : Leading Aircraftman

OTHER

ATA: Air Transport Auxiliary
CO : Commander
DFC : Distinguished Flying Cross
DFM : Distinguished Flying Medal
DSO : Distinguished Service Order
Eva. : Evaded
ORB : Operational Record Book
OTU : Operational Training Unit
PoW : Prisoner of War
PAF: Polish Air Force
RAF : Royal Air Force
RAAF : Royal Australian Air Force
RCAF : Royal Canadian Air Force
RNZAF : Royal New Zealand Air Force
SAAF : South African Air Force
s/d: Shot down
Sqn : Squadron
† : Killed

CODENAMES - OFFENSIVE OPERATIONS - FIGHTER COMMAND

CIRCUS:
Bombers heavily escorted by fighters, the purpose being to bring enemy fighters into combat.

RAMROD:
Bombers escorted by fighters, the primary aim being to destroy a target.

RANGER:
Large formation freelance intrusion over enemy territory with aim of wearing down enemy figthers.

RHUBARD:
Freelance fighter sortie against targets of opportunity.

ROADSTEAD:
Dive bombing and low level attacks on enemy ships at sea or in harbour

RODEO:
A fighter sweep without bombers.

SWEEP:
An offensive flight by fighters designed to draw up and clear the enemy from the sky.

THE BREWSTER BUFFALO MK. I

The Brewster Buffalo was born as the Brewster F2A for the United States Navy. It was the first monoplane fighter to be introduced into USN service. It first flew in December 1937 and the first variant, the F2A-1, was powered by a 940hp R-1820 engine and armed with four 0.50-in machine guns, but most were sold to Finland in favour of later delivery of the updated F2A-2. Indeed, a more powerful variant had been developed with a 1200 hp R-1820 engine and a redesigned rudder. It was offered, as a land-based export variant, as the Brewster 339. At the end of the thirties, with war approaching, many European countries were seeking new equipment, particularly modern fighters, and the Brewster looked promising. When war was declared in September 1939, requirements were drastically accelerated and the UK and Belgium were the first to place orders in January (120) and February 1940 (40) respectively. For the British, the Brewster 339 was not an obvious option as they were already producing two excellent fighters, the Hawker Hurricane and the Supermarine Spitfire, that were far superior to the American design. The Brewster fighter was initially rejected by the British Purchase Commission for this reason. However, the Air Ministry soon realised that production of both Hurricanes and Spitfires would not be enough to meet the RAF's increasing demands and the acquisition of foreign fighters was therefore seriously considered. By the end of 1939, all American manufacturers were overloaded and delivery delays repeatedly extended. Large orders could only be placed with the manufacturers not yet overloaded. The Brewster Corporation was one such manufacturer. Therefore, the Brewster 339 was the only suitable option and appeared to be a good alternative that left Hurricanes or Spitfires to theatres where the RAF was already engaged. So, while the RAF rejected the type for service in Europe and the Middle East, the Brewster 339 was deployed to the Far East where things were still quiet. Furthermore, ordering the Brewster Buffalo in small, but sufficient, quantities allowed the concentration of aircraft and spare parts in the same place and not spread across the United Kingdom. The other reason, which was to prove false, was that the Buffalo was thought good enough when compared to Japanese fighters. This idea was not based on a serious study as the British were not very interested in the Japanese aircraft industry and what they did know was superficial and mostly incorrect.

The British ordered the Brewster 339E (to become the Buffalo Mk.I in RAF service) in two batches, the first (already mentioned) of 120 aircraft with serials **W8131 to W8250**, followed by another fifty in July 1940 (**AN168-AN217**). Other than the first three

Three views (this page and the following) of the first Brewster B-339E W8131 (Buffalo Mk.I) before it was shipped to the UK for evaluation. Only three of the 170 RAF aircraft ordered went to Europe, the remaining production Buffaloes being sent to the Far East directly from the US. The registration NX417B was temporary to allow test flights and acceptance trials in the US. The United States was neutral at the time.

AS430, 'Brewster Fighter 339' as it was officially denominated, was a former Belgian B-339B and is seen here during testing at A&AAE during the Battle of Britain. The Belgian B-339 specifications were too different for the airframes to be considered Buffalo Mk.Is by the RAF and all except this one, converted to an instructional airframe in October 1940, went to the Fleet Air Arm.

Buffaloes, which were sent to the UK for trials, the other 167 aircraft all found their way to the Far East, deliveries taking place between February and August 1941. Buffalo W8131 joined the fleet from the UK in November. In the UK, disappointment was great as the trials conducted proved the type's performance was not as expected. This was caused by the increased weight required by the British, a factor made worse by the installation of a Wright Cyclone R-1820-G105 developing 1100hp instead of the 1200hp of the US model. The top speed and ceiling were therefore much less than the F2A-2 and, indeed, the B-339E was the heaviest of all the export versions (the RAF had had the opportunity to compare a Belgian B-339B diverted to the UK after Belgium collapsed). Furthermore, this extra weight also caused some instability. The bright side was the armament of four 0.50-in machine guns. The 0.50-in was a very powerful and efficient weapon, but was not widespread in the RAF at the time. Despite the known issues, the British could have requested Brewster to make some improvements, or perform some local mods, but nothing was done due to lack of time and money and the assumption that the Buffalo would still perform well against the Japanese. The RAF in the Far East split its Buffaloes into two batches. The main one (133 aircraft) was assigned to Malaya for squadrons mainly based at Singapore, while

Another 'Brewster Fighter 339', AS426, undergoing testing in the spring of 1941 and was not transferred to the Fleet Air Arm. This aircraft performed many tests and trials and eventually became a ground instructional airframe in March 1942.

31 were reserved for a single squadron based in Burma (No. 67), that number being enough to fully equip the squadron and cover attrition. The aircraft sent to Burma are known to be W8203, W8204, W8213, W8215, W8220, W8228, W8229, W8233, W8239, W8240, W8241, W8243, W8244-W8250 (7), AN168, AN169, AN182, AN190-AN193 (4), AN200, AN202, AN214, AN216 and AN217. The first batch of sixteen was despatched from Singapore (151 MU) in July 1941, followed by four Buffaloes in August, six in September and five in November. It seems that all but three were eventually erected. It must also be said that the United Kingdom inherited the balance of the Belgian order. Of the forty aircraft ordered, 33 reached the UK between July and September 1940. On 20 June 1940, the Belgian government in exile signed the aircraft over to the UK. Upon arrival they received the serials AS410-AS430 (21), AX810-AX820 (11) and BB450. The Belgian aircraft, the B-339E, were different to the British model and, therefore, after evaluation, were not incorporated into the Buffalo Mk.I fleet. They remained as the 'Brewster Fighter 339' and never received the 'Buffalo' denomination. Three aircraft were even sent to No. 71 (Eagle) Squadron, a unit manned by American pilots, in October 1940, but they were soon rejected after two weeks with the squadron, sealing the fate of this batch. At the same time, seeking modernisation, the Fleet Air Arm showed an early interest in taking on the aircraft. The B-339Bs were finally handed over to the FAA in November 1940.

Left and below: Most of the ex-Belgian B-339Bs were sent to Egypt where they equipped 805 Naval Air Squadron of the FAA. They served from land bases only until 1942. At left is AS420 and below is AX815.

Victories - confirmed or probable claims: 20.0

First operational sortie:
09.12.41
Last operational sortie:
??.03.42

Number of sorties: *n/k*

Total aircraft written-off: 30

Aircraft lost on operations: 26
Aircraft lost in accidents: 4

Squadron code letters:
RD

COMMANDING OFFICERS

S/L Robert A. MILWARD	RAF No. 37201	RAF	14.07.41	14.01.42
S/L Jack BRANDT	RAF No. 39849	RAF	14.01.42	...

SQUADRON USAGE

This unit was re-formed at Kallang on 11 March 1941. It had had a previous existence in WW1 and was manned by Australians as No. 1 Squadron Australian Flying Corps. The squadron was to be the first Buffalo unit in the RAF. Formation was slow even though the first Buffalo, W8141, arrived on the 14th. Three days later, W8135 and W8138 were included in the squadron's inventory, followed by W8143 the next day. At the same time some personnel were sent to Seletar to be instructed on the Buffalo. At the end of the month, two more aircraft were added (W8144 and W8148).

In April, the squadron was split into two flights: A Flight, under the command of F/O D.J.C. Pinckney, and B Flight, led by P/O J.S. Wigglesworth. More pilots arrived and more Buffaloes were taken on strength (W8150, W8153, W8156, W8161, W8190 and W8191, but W8141 returned to Seletar). Progressively, the number of daily training hours increased and the first thirty-hour inspection was undertaken on W8135 on the 21st. However, the Buffalo was only good for training as the radio-telephone and oxygen systems were not yet installed in each aircraft on hand. The first truly operational Buffalo, and therefore the first in the RAF, was W8147. In all, A Flight flew 71 hours in April and B Flight flew 150. In May, the squadron, still with no official CO, increased in size. Buffaloes W8168, W8173, W8175, W8185, W8193, W8195,

A Flight, of 67 Sqn, at Mingaladon in December 1941, posing in front of Buffalo W8243/RD-B. In the cockpit is Sgt C.V. Bargh and on the wing is P/O C. McG. Simpson. Standing, left to right, are Sergeants G.A. Williams, E.E. Pedersen and E.L. Sadler, F/O P.M. Bingham-Wallis, P/O G.S. Sharp, and Sergeants K.A. Rutherford and J. Macpherson. With the exception of Bingham-Wallis, every pilot was a member of the RNZAF.
(C.V. Bargh via P. Sortehaug)

A line of 67 Sqn Buffaloes at Mindagalon with RD-H in the foreground.

W8198 and W8200 were collected from Seletar, while more pilots arrived, so, on 26 May, the squadron had twenty aircraft on hand (sixteen plus four in reserve). In May, 172.5 hours were flown. The first accidents occurred in June. While the misfortunes of W8153 (3 June), W8185 (11 June) and W8191 (12 June) were not considered major, it was not the case for the recently arrived W8146 which crashed on the 21st after an engine failure at 300 feet. The pilot, Sgt C.V. Bargh (RNZAF), emerged unscathed, but the aircraft was too damaged to repair. As the training program intensified so did the risk of accidents. In all 264 hours were flown in June. On 14 July, the newly appointed OC, S/L R.A. Milward, arrived at the squadron. A recipient of the DFC, he was an experienced pilot who had fought with No. 30 Squadron in the Middle East and Greece. That month, the number of hours flown was close to 420, with only a single minor accident on the negative side (W8177 suffered an undercarriage failure on the 26th). The number of hours dropped to 266 in August with another minor accident (W8148 on 22nd), but increased to 432 in September for the cost of three wrecked Buffaloes – W8190 on the 8th, W8144 on the 19th, and W8161 on the 23rd. The latter was damaged in a collision with a Blenheim and obliged to make a forced landing. The two other crashed on landing at Kallang (W8144) and Seletar (W8190).

General flying ceased on 4 October, the squadron now to be based in Burma at Mingaladon where sixteen Buffaloes from No. 60 Squadron were waiting to be handed over. In November, 330 hours were flown during which another two minor accidents were reported. First, on 12 November, W8247 burst a tyre on landing and the undercarriage collapsed. The Buffalo was repaired and returned to the squadron on 8 December. Six days later, it was the turn of AN169, but the extent of the damage suffered is not known with certainty. No further trace of usage by the squadron was found. There is some doubt as to whether it flew again. The aircraft may have been too damaged to be economically repaired, or repairs were undertaken but never completed due to the desperate times that were to come. It may have been used for parts to repair other Buffaloes damaged in combat.

Between 1 and 7 December no flying was carried out as all aircraft were grounded for inspection of valves and tappets. Maintenance crews worked in shifts to carry out the work. During that period, the international situation deteriorated considerably and war with Japan appeared imminent to many. On the 8th, the squadron was informed that Japan had begun its attacks on Malaya, Thailand and the Philippines. The squadron immediately assumed its role in the defence of Rangoon and two sections were kept at readiness throughout daylight hours. At the same time ground crew intensified the inspection work to return as many aircraft as possible to service. Nothing happened on the 9th, but the next day one unidentified aircraft was sighted flying very high over the aerodrome. The section on patrol failed to intercept it. On the 12th, two Buffaloes escorted a Blenheim on an uneventful photographic reconnaissance over Thailand. Japanese reconnaissance flights continued to fly over the area, but none could be intercepted due to the unreliability of the plotting system. So far, Japanese forces were too far from the Buffaloes' area of operations to expect any combat. Every day, however, 67 continued dispatching three aircraft to Mergui, used as an advance base, relieving the three aircraft already there. On the 17th, four Buffaloes were sent to Mergui. One of the newcomers was camera-equipped (W8241 – flown F/O P.M. Bingham-Wallis) and its task was to make reconnaissance flights between Victoria Point and the east coast of Thailand where Japanese activity had been reported. Following a technical problem, the op had to be delayed for a day, but nothing was eventually found. In the afternoon, another photographic sortie was carried out, flown by Bingham-Wallis, to take photos of Prachan and Girikham airfield in Thailand. The photographs showed a number of aircraft dispersed around the perimeter of the airfield and in front of a hangar. Consequently, an attack was planned for the morning of the 21st. Therefore, three more Buffaloes, led by the CO,

arrived to Mergui to join those already there. The attack was regarded as successful in that the attacking aircraft left a fuel dump on fire and five aircraft destroyed on the ground. On arriving back to Mergui, Bingham-Wallis was instructed to carry out a reconnaissance of the area around Chumphon and Victoria Point and to strafe targets of opportunity. Sergeant G.A. Williams (RNZAF) acted as escort. They eventually strafed a train, in southern Thailand, traveling south with reinforcements. They returned to Tavoy for refuelling before going to back to Mingaladon in the evening.

The relative calm came to an end on the 23rd. That day the Japanese attacked Rangoon and its airfields with more than seventy bombers (Ki-21s or Ki-30s) plus escorts. The Japanese formation was detected just before 10.00. About fifteen Buffaloes, and a dozen Curtiss Warhawks from the American Volunteer Group (AVG), managed to reach 20,000 feet before engaging the Japanese. The results were better than expected. Sergeant G.A. Williams, who was one of the first to engage, claimed one Ki-27 fighter shot down and another as a probable (without counting four others damaged). Sergeant C.V. Bargh also claimed a Ki-21 as probably destroyed, but his aircraft was shot full of holes. He managed to evade his attackers and flew out to sea where he regained height. His windscreen was covered in oil, so he calmly removed his flying boot, opened the cockpit and wiped the screen clean with his sock before continuing his search for the bombers. At 17,000 feet he was joined by Sgt E.H. Beable (RNZAF) and together they dived onto a formation below. Bargh claimed one bomber shot down, last seen in a dive with its fuselage alight. Other pilots opened their score too. Flying Officer J.E. Lambert claimed one Japanese bomber destroyed (he mistook it for a He111!), while F/O J.S. Wigglesworth, a Battle of Britain veteran who also identified a He111, was credited with a probable, and Sgt K.A. Rutherford (RNZAF) another damaged. Pilot Officer G.S. Sharp (RNZAF) fired one long burst, presumably at Ki-30s, before being engaged by fighters. He evaded and returned to base to be credited with one damaged Ki-30. Sergeant W.Christiansen attacked a formation of bombers, which he also identified as Heinkels, and selected one. He flew a front quarter attack, breaking away with his windscreen covered with oil; the bomber was claimed as probably destroyed. On the ground, damage was not as bad as expected despite the operations room being destroyed (injuring personnel including S/L Milward) along with two Buffaloes. Sadly, the squadron lost two ground crew, AC1s L.R. Lintott and W.J. King. The following day was quiet, but the Japanese returned in force on the 25th with about 100 bombers and a strong escort. Due to the lack of a proper operations room, no adequate warning was given, but twelve Buffaloes were sent to patrol: one section at 12,000 feet (F/L J. Brandt), the other (F/L D.J.C. Pinckney) at 17,000 feet, and two aircraft flying 3000 feet higher. It did not take long before those two Buffaloes (F/O P.M. Bingham-Wallis and Sgt G.A. Williams) spotted two formations of bombers. They warned the rest of the squadron and both went into attack the first formation. Bingham-Wallis sealed the fate of one Ki-21 after his second pass, the aircraft crashing into the sea, then a Ki-43 as they fired at each other. Williams managed to get into a good position and saw the Ki-43 out of control after he fired at it, but he had no time to see if the fighter crashed. He was credited with a probable. In the meantime, the other Buffaloes were far from inactive, but did not fare so well. Flight Lieutenant Pinckney did everything he could to evade two Japanese fighters and saw an aircraft burning in a paddy field. After five minutes he lost his attackers and returned to where he saw the aircraft burning, He recognised it as New Zealander Sgt J. Macpherson's Buffalo AN216. Macpherson was not the only one to lose his life in the action. Flying Officer J.E. Lambert and Sergeants E.B. Hewitt (RNZAF) and R.P. McNabb did not return. However, the squadron made more claims and several pilots filed combat reports: Sgt C.V. Bargh (one Ki-21 probable), P/O G.S. Sharp, who landed a seriously damaged Buffalo, (one Ki-27 probable), Sgt E.E. Pederson (two Ki-27 damaged), F/L J. Brandt (one Ki-27 confirmed), Sgt E.H. Beable (one Ki-27 probable and another damaged), and Sgt J.G. Finn (one Ki-27 destroyed). The losses could have been worse as Lambert and Sharp received hits to the armour plate on their seatbacks, something not all of the Buffaloes had been fitted with yet. In all, the squadron destroyed one bomber and three fighters, probably destroyed four fighters, and claimed three more damaged. The Japanese were able to destroy two more Buffaloes parked in dispersals. Three other Buffaloes (believed to be W8215, AN200 and AN217) awaiting assembly were also destroyed. The aerodrome was fully operational at the end of the next day, but little flying was carried out before the end of the month with just a few patrols on the 29th. The squadron logged just over 500 hours in December. At that time the Buffalo fleet in Burma had, in just two actions, already been reduced by a third!

In the beginning of January 1942, the Buffaloes performed only a handful of defensive patrols. On the 9th, in conjunction with four AVG P-40s, six Buffaloes were dispatched to strafe Tak airfield. Flight Lieutenants Brandt and Pinckney claimed two Type 97 aircraft destroyed on the ground, while another four were damaged by the other pilots. That night the Japanese bombed Rangoon and Mingaladon. Flight Lieutenant Pinckney and F/O Bingham-Wallis decided to try an interception, but no contact was made. The next morning, S/L R.A. Milward led three other Buffaloes (Sergeants K.A. Rutherford, E.E. Pederson and E.L. Sadler all RNZAF)

Two side views of Buffalo W8245, one of the six of its type to survive the Burma Campaign.

Sgt 'Ketchil' Bargh posing proudly on the Japanese aircraft he shot down on 24 January 1942. *(C.V. Bargh via P. Sortehaug)*

to attack Mesoht airfield, strafing troops seen in the area and destroying two single-engine aircraft. Pressure on the Japanese continued the following week and, not totally recovered from his wounds sustained on 23 December, Milward had to relinquish command to F/L Brandt. Milward was promoted to wing commander and posted to Air HQ. During that week, the Buffaloes mounted some preventative patrols, but also flew reconnaissance sorties. On 13 January 1942, P/O P.M. Brewer (RNZAF) flew to Don Mueang airfield, 150 miles north of Bangkok, and then to Tavoy where he encountered a two-seater aircraft. He climbed above it unobserved and made his first attack from out of the sun. The aircraft took no evasive action and was set on fire. It headed for the Thai border and an explosion was seen as it entered the hills. The next day, F/L Pinckney led two other Buffaloes to Mesoht airfield where they set a large aircraft taxiing across the airfield on fire. It soon exploded after the last pass by Pinckney. On the 15th, it was the turn of F/L Brandt and Sergeants Christensen and Sadler to claim seven aircraft damaged at Prachuab Giri Khan airfield. On the 19th, two Buffaloes were involved in a dogfight with Ki-27s while escorting Blenheims of No. 113 Squadron, the escort carried out in conjunction with AVG P-40s. While the combat was fierce, no claims were reported. The following day, two Buffaloes were ordered to undertake a reconnaissance to Raheng during the morning and to refuel at Moulmein on the return flight. Having completed the reconnaissance, P/O P.M. Brewer and Sgt J. Finn were almost ready to take off again from Moulmein when a number of Ki-27s caught them by surprise. They attempted to get off the ground, but were immediately attacked. While they got airborne, it was only briefly as they were both shot down and killed. From 23 January onwards, the RAF introduced the Hurricane to Burma, just in time as the Buffaloes and pilots, after a month of intense flying, were reaching their limits. The Buffalo, however, was far from being withdrawn as all forces available had to try to stop the Japanese. That day, two aircraft were scrambled to intercept a reconnaissance aircraft, indicating an impending air raid on Mingaladon, escorted by Ki-27s. They were tasked to go after this lone aircraft, but before they could do so they had to face the mass of escorting fighters. Flight Lieutenant Pinckney was shot down and killed near Pegu (receiving a DFC for his action the following June), but his loss was balanced by the claim of one Ki-27 destroyed by Sgt Christiansen. A third Buffalo flown by P/O A.A. Cooper (RNZAF) joined the mêlée with AVG P-40s. Cooper made a claim for one Ki-27 damaged. The next day, only half a dozen Buffaloes could be dispatched to face another raid. Sergeant E.L. Sadler made two attacks on a Ki-21 that immediately dropped out of the formation and crashed in flames. His next attack also set fire to another one that was eventually claimed by two other pilots of the AVG who finished it off. Pilot Officer Cooper fired a long burst into a bomber that blew up, but was hit by return fire and his engine began to emit smoke and flames. He dived steeply with switches off and blew the fire out. Finally, Sgt Vic Bargh claimed his second victory when his victim's wings and engine parted from the fuselage under the weight of his fire. It was to be the swansong for the Buffalo in Burma, even though there were about a dozen Brewsters available (of which an estimated number 4-6 were serviceable at any one time). It became more and more difficult to repair the aircraft damaged as parts were almost non-existent and maintenance was not easy to perform in the prevailing conditions. Some damaged aircraft, therefore, served to provide parts for others. The situation worsened on the 2 February when F/O J. Wigglesworth lost his life taking off from Taungoo at the head of a section of Buffaloes tasked to strafe Chiang Mai airfield. The engine of his Buffalo cut as he became airborne and the aircraft force-landed in a paddy field where it turned over. The windscreen shattered and a fragment pierced Wigglesworth's skull, killing him instantly. Maintenance shortcomings might have been the main cause of the accident. Anyhow, the Hurricane had taken over the job and the Buffaloes were used less from the beginning of February. It is difficult to confirm, but operational activity remained low and it seems reconnaissance flights were the main task given to 67. The Buffaloes known to still be operational in February were W8228, W8233, W8243, W8245, W8246, W8250, AN168, AN191 and AN214. On 19 February, when Rangoon was about to be captured, 67 Squadron destroyed three unserviceable Buffaloes and the remaining airworthy fighters were flown to Magwe. Soon after, 67 Squadron pilots were converted to Hurricanes and flew on either type depending on availability. In any case, operational flights by Buffaloes became less and less common. The last major action involving Buffaloes took place on 4 March when four aircraft participated in a strafing stack on Chiang Mai airfield. On return, the formation landed at Namsang to refuel, but Buffalo AN168 hit a truck and was damaged beyond repair. While the pilot was unhurt, a lack of documentation prevents identifying who he was. Three days later, AN191 was wrecked while taking off for a patrol over Army convoys. The engine started to miss at 50 feet and cut out altogether at 100 feet. The pilot, F/L Bingham-Wallis, had no choice but to make a forced-landing in a pond, sealing the fate of the Buffalo.

On 10 March, 67 Squadron was at last relieved and S/L Brandt led the six remaining flyable Buffaloes (W8228, W8243, W8245, W8246, W8250 and AN214) to Akyab and then Dum Dum. Within a couple of weeks 67 Squadron was completely re-equipped with Hurricanes.

Claims - 67 Squadron (Confirmed and Probable)

Date	Pilot	SN	Origin	Type	Serial	Code	Nb	Cat.
23.12.41	Sgt Gordon A. **Williams**	NZ405356	RNZAF	Ki-27	**W8245**	RD-D	1.0	C
				Ki-27			1.0	P
	Sgt Charles V. **Bargh**	NZ40960	RNZAF	Ki-21	**AN168**		1.0	C
				Ki-21			1.0	P
	F/O John E. **Lambert**	RAF No. 40924	RAF	Ki-21	**AN214**		1.0	C
	F/O John S. **Wigglesworth**	RAF No. 42930	RAF	Ki-21			1.0	P
	Sgt William **Christiansen**	NZ40964	RNZAF	Ki-21			1.0	P
25.12.41	F/O Peter M. **Bingham-Wallis**	RAF No. 40878	RAF	Ki-21	**W8245**	RD-D	1.0	C
				Ki-43			1.0	C
	Sgt Gordon A. **Williams**	NZ405356	RNZAF	Ki-43	**W8228**		1.0	P
	Sgt Charles V. **Bargh**	NZ40960	RNZAF	Ki-27	**AN202**		1.0	P
	P/O Geoff S. **Sharp**	NZ403476	RNZAF	Ki-27			1.0	P
	F/J Jack **Brandt**	RAF No. 39849	RAF	Ki-27	**W8213**		1.0	C
	Sgt Edward H. **Beable**	NZ404935	RNZAF	Ki-27	**W8247**		1.0	P
	Sgt John G. **Finn**	NZ404859	RNZAF	Ki-27	**W8240**		1.0	C
13.01.42	P/O Paul M. **Brewer**	NZ402565	RNZAF	Ki-15	**W8229**		1.0	C
23.01.42	Sgt William **Christiansen**	NZ40964	RNZAF	Ki-27	**W8203**		1.0	C
24.01.42	Sgt Edward L. **Sadler**	NZ402901	RNZAF	Ki-21			1.0	C
	P/O Anthony A. **Cooper**	NZ41467	RNZAF	Ki-21	**W8241**		1.0	C
	Sgt Charles V. **Bargh**	NZ40960	RNZAF	Ki-27	**W8250**	RD-E	1.0	C

Total: 20.0

NB: The basic documentation was destroyed during the retreat from Burma and the details of these claims are mainly based on pilot's logbooks that survived.

Left: Sergeant G.A. Williams made two claims over Japanese aircraft and was one of the first to do so. He continued to serve with 67 Sqn until February 1944 and by the end of the war was flying Corsairs with 24 Sqn RNZAF in Bougainville in the Solomon Islands.
Right: Sergeant W.J. Christiansen posing in front of a Buffalo. He was also among the few to make a claim in Burma. While he survived the campaign, he was later posted missing in action on 9 April 1943 while still serving with 67 Sqn.
(G.S. Sharp via P. Sortehaug)

Summary of the aircraft lost on Operations - 67 Squadron

Date	Pilot	S/N	Origin	Serial	Code	Fate
25.12.41	Sgt John **MACPHERSON**	NZ41486	RNZAF	**AN216**		†
	F/O John E. **LAMBERT**	RAF No. 40924	RAF	**W8220**	RD-V	†
	Sgt Edward B. **HEWITT**	NZ405269	RNZAF	**W8248**		†
	Sgt Ronald P. **MCNABB**	NZ404393	RNZAF	**W8206**		†
20.01.42	P/O Paul M. **BREWER**	NZ402565	RNZAF	**W8229**		†
	Sgt John G. **FINN**	NZ404859	RNZAF	**W8240**		†
23.01.42	F/L David J.C. **PINCKNEY**	RAF No. 72520	RAF	**W8239**	RD-A	†
06.02.42	F/O John S. **WIGGLESWORTH**	RAF No. 42930	RAF	**W8213**		†
04.03.42	*Details missing*	?	?	**AN168**		-
07.03.42	F/O Peter M. **BINGHAM-WALLIS**	RAF No. 40878	RAF	**AN191**	RD-H	-

Total: 10[1]

[1] To this total, it should be added the aircraft destroyed on the ground - see text

Date	Pilot	S/N	Origin	Serial	Code	Fate
21.06.41	Sgt Charles V. BARGH	NZ40960	RNZAF	W8146	RD-D	-
08.09.41	Sgt Eric E. PEDERSEN	NZ403984	RNZAF	W8190	RD-F	-
19.09.41	Sgt Eric E. PEDERSEN	NZ403984	RNZAF	W8144	RD-C	-
23.09.41	F/O John S. WIGGLESWORTH	RAF No. 42930	RAF	W8161		-

Total: 4[1]

[1] Only the accidents which took place at Singapore are known.

Three other pilots of 67 Sqn in December 1941. Left to right: : Sgt R.P. McNabb, F/O P.M. Bingham-Wallis and F/O J.E. Lambert. Only Bingham-Wallis survived the war while McNabb and Lambert were killed over Burma on the same day.
(G.S. Sharp via P. Sortehaug)

Victories - confirmed or probable claims: **24.0**

Number of sorties: *ca.***200**

First operational sortie:
08.12.41
Last operational sortie:
04.07.44

Total aircraft written-off: **13**

Aircraft lost on operations: **13**
Aircraft lost in accidents: **-**

Squadron code letters:
WP

COMMANDING OFFICERS

S/L Gerald B.M. BELL	RAF No. 37002	RAF	12.03.41	06.12.41
S/L Frank J. HOWELL	RAF No. 39612	RAF	06.12.41	...

SQUADRON USAGE

The second unit to be formed on Buffaloes was 243 Squadron, with the official date being 12 March. Five officers and 130 personnel of other ranks had disembarked and proceeded immediately to Kallang the previous day. Command was given to S/L G.B.M. Bell and the two flight commanders were F/O T.A. Vigors DFC, who had fought during the Battle of Britain with No. 222 Squadron, and F/O J. Mansel-Lewis, also a Battle of Britain veteran, but with No. 92 Squadron. The first Buffaloes (W8139/B, W8134/M and W8142/N) were collected the next day and were followed by W8137/C the day after. By the end of the month, W8140, W8145 and W8149 had also been collected. The squadron was rocked on 4 April when F/O J. Mansel-Lewis perished when the Blenheim he was a passenger of crashed. He was replaced by F/O R. Bows from 18 April 1941 onwards. During the month, while training had begun, more Buffaloes arrived with W8154 and W8155 added to the squadron's inventory. One of these aircraft was the replacement for W8149 which had slid into an irrigation ditch on the aerodrome on the 8th. The Kiwi pilot, P/O E.A. Pevreal, escaped uninjured, but the aircraft was at least 70% damaged and only good for scrap. On 5 May Buffaloes W8192 and W8194 were collected, but W8194 was to have a short career with the RAF as it was destroyed a week later after an engine failure, crashing in the canal 100 yards from Kallang aerodrome. The New Zealand pilot, Sgt A.R.P. Paul, escaped injury. The unit took some time to reach a normal squadron establishment, the next Buffaloes arriving on the 19th and 20th (W8182, W8187/R, W8189/Q), then W8164, W8181/P, W8199/S on the 23rd. Two days later, W8162, W8164/J and W8179 were taken on charge. As for personnel, more young pilots, mostly from New Zealand, were posted in. Training continued and more aircraft were lost during the summer: W8182 on 23 July, P/O F.W.J. Okaden (RNZAF) being obliged to

The CO, S/L Frank Howell, was a pre-war RAF officer. Enlisted on a short service commission in March 1937, he was serving in Egypt when war broke out. Recalled to the UK, he became a flight commander with 609 Sqn at the end of 1939. He participated in the actions over Dunkirk, and then the Battle of Britain, and received the DFC in October 1940. In 1941 he was given command of the newly-formed 118 Sqn before being sent overseas in the autumn with a Bar to his DFC. He was eventually captured on 15 February 1942. He survived the harsh conditions of his captivity and continued to serve the RAF before being killed in a flying accident in May 1948.

A group photo of 243 Squadron B Flight pilots with F/Sgt G. Mothersdale at the far right. At the rear, left to right: Sgt J. Oliver, F/L R. Bows, P/O J. Cranstone, and Sergeants N.B. Rankin and G. Fisken.
Middle row, left to right: Sgt V. Arthur, F/O M.H. Holder, P/O T.B. Marra.
Seated: Sergeants A.J. Lawrence and B.K. Baber. All but Bows and Holder were members of the RNZAF. In a few weeks, Oliver and Arthur would both be posted killed in action. *(T.B. Marra via P. Sortehaug)*

make a forced landing 70 yards offshore and seven miles north-east of Singapore town (he was not injured), and the undercarriage of W8134 collapsed on landing on 16 August (Sgt J.B. Oliver - RNZAF). At the end of July, three pilots with sufficient training, F/O T.A. Vigors, and Pilot Officers E.A. Pevreal and P.M. Holder, were sent on detachment to Kota Bharu. Their task was to intercept and, if possible, force down any unidentified aircraft flying over British territory or territorial waters. Instructions were given not to fire unless fired upon first and to pursue unidentified aircraft as far as the Thai border. The detachment ceased at the beginning of September and the machines and personnel retuned to Kallang. In November, P/O G.L. Bonham crashed in W8154, but was unhurt. That would be the last write-off for the peacetime period. Two days before the Japanese invasion, S/L Bell was called to command RAF Kallang and relinquished command to S/L F. Howell DFC and Bar. The squadron could count 28 pilots in its ranks, with all but five being New Zealanders. Of the other five, one was Australian. By that time, four more Buffaloes had been taken on: W8221/X, W8242/K, AN196/W and AN197.

On 7 December, Kota Bharu was attacked by Japanese soldiers who had landed from troopships. The squadron had a detachment there of two pilots (Pilot Officers M.H. Holder and R.S. Shield RNZAF), seven airmen, and Buffaloes W8196 and W8221. The next day, they were ordered to take off at 06.30 to strafe barges reported being towed up the Kelantan towards Kota Bharu town. Both made strafing passes, but Holder's Buffalo, W8196, was hit by small arms fire, making it difficult for him to control when landing back to Kota Bharu. He could not avoid a crashed Hudson and collided with it, causing extensive damage to the mainplane of the Buffalo. It was, if we believe the ORB, written off. In the meantime, Shield encountered a formation of nine Ki-21s and gave chase. He positioned his aircraft well and opened fire, but, after one burst, three of his guns jammed, leaving him with a single gun that also jammed after two further bursts. The squadron also sent a Buffalo, flown by Sgt C.B. Wareham (RNZAF), on a photographic reconnaissance early that day. The Kota Bharu detachment retuned by rail to Kallang while Buffalo W8221 was flown back by F/O M.H. Holder, who took with him some photographs for the air headquarters. Over the next few days, the main occupation of 243 was carrying out patrols from Kallang. On the 10th, Sergeants J.B. Oliver and N.B. Rankin, both RNZAF, were sent on a recce of Kuantan aerodrome and surroundings. Several white smoke fires were observed to the north-east of town. The Buffaloes circled the aerodrome at 500 feet, which appeared to still be serviceable, and noted a burnt out Blenheim on the south-west corner. The same day, the squadron dispatched a single Buffalo, flown by F/L M. Garden, to inspect the damage to the battlecruiser HMS *Repulse* and the battleship HMS *Prince of Wales* following reports they had been attacked by Japanese aircraft. There was nothing to report other than the two ships were about to sink. Patrols flown later that day could only confirm the disastrous demise of the ships. Soon after, a detachment of four Buffaloes led by F/O Holder was sent to Ipoh as reinforcements. On 13 December, Penang was subjec-

Twelve Brewster Buffalo Mk Is of No. 243 Squadron in flight over the Malayan jungle in formations of three, accompanied by a Bristol Blenheim Mark IV of No. 34 Squadron. Note that some aircraft have still to receive their squadron code letters. The aircraft with the individual letters which could be identified are: W8181/WP-P, W8142/WP-N, W8184/WP-G, W8139/WP-B, W8242/WP-K, W8196/WP-U, AN196/WP-W and W8178/WP-Y

ted to another attack during the morning by an estimated thirty bombers. The Ipoh detachment managed to put up two Buffaloes. Sergeant Geoff Fisken engaged the Japanese bombers and made his first claim (and, therefore, 243's first claim) by diving on, and shooting down, an Army 97 (credited as probable). During the rest of the month, squadron activity was sparse and, for all of December, 109 sorties, mostly defensive patrols, were flown by 243, including three more reconnaissance flights flown by Sgt Wareham in a specially modified Buffalo. On 3 January, 243 was called to carry out convoy patrols but the section made of P/O G.L. Bonham and Sgt C.F. Powell got lost in cloud and were separated from the rest of their flight. While Bonhma returned on the last drops of his fuel but Sgt Powell didn't have this chance and was obliged to make a force-landing short of fuel and was seriously injured in the process. Despiste his injuries, he managed to reach civilisation the next day and was taken to the local hospital for treatment.

Things remained then quiet until 10 January 1942. In the early morning, radar operators at Singapore plotted the course of a single reconnaissance aircraft as it approached the island. The fighter controller vectored two Buffaloes from the squadron (Sergeants B.S. Wipiti and C.T. Kronk – both RNZAF) to intercept. The Japanese aircraft, a Ki-46, was initially sighted by Sergeant Wipiti who dived on to its tail to fire one long burst, gaining strikes on one engine and slowing the aircraft down. Joined by Sgt Kronk (WP-A), the two New Zealanders chased the Ki-46 down, firing until it crashed in the jungle in southern Johore. The next day the weather was too bad and no significant air activity was carried out. However, on the 12th, the Japanese returned. The squadron scrambled too late. It had already patrolled for about 45 minutes, and had returned to base and were about to land, when the Japanese raided Tengah. Luckily the bombs fell wide, but the Buffaloes quickly refuelled and took off. The Japanese didn't even try to intercept them. Later in the afternoon, there was another scramble when seventy Ki-27s returned, this time engaging 243 Squadron. Leading A Flight, F/L Garden, in W8139/B, attacked nine Ki-27s head on in misty cloud and claimed one destroyed as it closed on him. Over the next few minutes, his tally increased by two more claims, one destroyed and one probably destroyed. He was then attacked, his Buffalo sustaining significant damage, and forced to break off, the aircraft vibrating severely. He managed to put it on the ground but, as the Buffalo came to a halt at the end of the runway, it slowly collapsed around him. The aircraft was a write-off. In the mean-

Buffalo W8134/WP-M seen during the summer of 1941. The final fate of this aircraft is not known. This aircraft was victim of an accident on 16 August 1941 when its undercarriage collapsed on landing, this kind of accident being usually fatal for a Buffalo. This aircraft was possibly still under repairs when the Japanese attacked Malaya.
(A. Thomas)

Squadron Leader Howell flanked by the two successful pilots who made the claim on 10 January 1942: Sergeants B. Wapiti and C. Kronk.
(Kronk family via P. Sortehaug)

time, B Flight was also facing the Ki-27s and F/O 'Blondie' Holder claimed two of them destroyed, with another being claimed by Sgt Geoff Fisken (W8147/O) in a head to head confrontation, both aircraft firing at one another. Fisken pulled up at the last moment and saw the Japanese fighter blow up underneath him. The explosion was so close that Fisken lost control and was put in to an inverted spin. He tried to evacuate his aircraft, but his oxygen mask remained connected to the cockpit, so he changed his mind and miraculously managed to recover from the spin and return to base. The Japanese shot down one of 243's pilots, Sgt 'Slim' Newman in W8137/C. He had made a forced landing at Kallan, but, shot in the stomach, sadly died. Other claims were made during the raid with P/O G.L. Bonham reporting one G3M destroyed and another damaged (in WP-F). He had discovered the formation after evading the Ki-27s by diving into cloud. A little bit later, sections of 243 Squadron were again scrambled, Sgt Max Greenslade claiming one Navy O damaged, while Sgt Russell Reynolds is believed to have submitted claims for two aircraft probably destroyed. What was definite was that 243 lost another pilot, Sgt Noel Rankin, shot down and killed by the Ki-27s. His parachute was later recovered from the sea.

The next day, the 13th, a second reinforcement convoy, carrying 51 crated Hurricanes and 24 pilots, was making its approach towards Keppel Harbour. A strong Japanese reaction was anticipated and all units were told to expect to defend the convoy. Besides the requisite convoy patrols, the Buffaloes had to contend with another raid on Singapore by light bombers escorted by many Ki-43s. The squadron scrambled to intercept the incoming raid despite heavy rain causing the formation to break up. Therefore, many interceptionss were made by single aircraft such as F/L Garden who, upon breaking cloud, surprised a Japanese fighter. While the latter saw him at the last moment and began evasive action, Garden was able to maintain contact and, with a long burst, crippled him. He saw the fighter dive to the ground. Other pilots made claims during this action. Pilot Officer N. Sharp claimed one fighter destroyed while Sergeants Pevreal and Kronk shared a probably destroyed claim over another. On the debit side, Sgt 'Russ' Reynolds, 19-years old, failed to return. Bad weather continued on the 14th and hampered the Japanese from attacking Singapore heavily. However, one Ki-46 was sent on a reconnaissance mission escorted by Navy A6M 'Zeros'. They met patrolling Buffaloes from 243 and 488 Squadrons and engaged. One 'Zero' was claimed by Sgt Fisken who initially reported a probable, but it was later confirmed destroyed. The opposing pilot was no slouch as Fisken returned with eighteen bullet holes in his aircraft. The next day, all squadrons scrambled as the enemy returned over Tengah and Sembawang to attack the aerodrome. The escorting fighters gave 243 a hard time and many Buffaloes were hit. However, on landing back at base, 243's tally had increased by one confirmed victory over a Ki-27 (P/O T.B. Marra) and one probable A6M 'Zero' shared by F/L Garden and Sgt R.A. Weber. Sergeant M.A. Greenslade claimed a Japanese bomber as damaged, but he could not press home this attack as his aircraft was hit by return fire. Pressure continued to increase over the two airfields of Singapore Island as the Japanese decided to eliminate the threat for good. The squadron was the only unit to score on the 16th with one probable 'Zero' claimed by Sgt Kronk while the CO sealed the fate of a recon-

naissance C5M when he spotted the aircraft and, approaching from the rear, fired one good burst. The enemy aircraft immediately went straight down, bursting into flames and, before it crashed, one wing parted company with the rest of the airframe. An attempt to carry out a reconnaissance flight over Mersing failed as the two pilots, Sgt G.B. Fisken and F/O M.H. Holder, lost each other in clouds and returned to base. The next day, 243 added five more victories shared by Holder and Fisken in an oustanding display of airmanship each pilot pilot downed a 'Nell' and shared the destruction of two more between them. On the 18th, six claims were made by six different pilots for no loss. However, five of the Buffaloes returned with varying degrees of damage. One of these was flown Sgt Kronk whose tail wheel was shot off. Pilot Officer T.B. Marra landed in W8143, but when he saw the extent of the damage to the aircraft, he realised that it would have been wiser to bale out. With the Buffalo so damaged, and the Allies' situation worsening, the mechanics did not have time to repair W8143, using it for spare parts instead. One pilot was wounded, P/O G.L. Bonham, with a bullet in his knee, but he managed to land his machine. On the morning of the 19th, 243 scrambled two sections of Buffaloes to help three Dutch Martin bombers being attacked by Japanese fighters, but they arrived too late. In the afternoon, the squadron was airborne again to try to help Buffaloes manned by the Australians on an offensive sweep in case they were intercepted by 'Zeros'. It was an uneventful flight for the unit. There was no raid that day. The squadron's strength had been whittled away to six Buffaloes, four in A Flight and two in B Flight, and eight unserviceable aircraft. The squadron expected to be reinforced by the recently arrived Hurricanes, but at that stage only eighteen of them were in the process of being assembled, the rest being held in reserve or for use as spare parts.

The reason why the Japanese didn't attack on the 19th became evident on the 20th when they made the heaviest raid so far experienced by Singapore. They had taken a day off to prepare. About eighty bombers approached mid-morning. The squadron scrambled to intercept, but the order came too late and they could not gain sufficient height to reach the first bombers. The escort took care of the Buffaloes with more than forty Japanese fighters preventing an interception of the bombers. Pilot Officer Gifford, flying his first sortie with 243, dived to escape an attack. The dive was so steep that the leading edge of the wings became distorted and the ailerons wrecked. Buffalo W8173 had probably made its last flight and it is doubtful that ground crews wasted any time trying to effect repairs. Later in the afternoon, four pilots led by F/L M. Garden found their way to Batu Pahat where Japanese bombers were caught attacking the aerodrome. Sergeant C.T. Kronk and P/O N.C. Sharp shot down one bomber each while Sgt V. Arthur claimed two more damaged (as did Garden). Sharp's Buffalo was damaged by return fire.

On the 21st, at first light, Garden led six Buffaloes on a sweep over the Batu Pahat-Parit Sulong area. They spotted and attacked two gunboats and several barges carrying Japanese soldiers. Later, while patrolling the area at 22,000 feet, another section of Buffaloes was bounced by an equal number of Ki-43s. Sergeant Wipiti was able to shoot down one of the Japanese in flames while Sgt Kronk claimed another as a probable. These claims were made without any loss, although F/L Garden's Buffalo was hit and returned with a large hole in the port wing. The Japanese came back in force later in the day. The squadron scrambled with all available aircraft, but, by the time they had gained sufficient height, the bombers were on their way home. After a couple of minutes they caught some isolated G4Ms, and F/L R. Bows, who was leading 243, ordered a head-on attack, but Navy 'Zeros' interfered. Nevertheless, Sgt 'Ginger' Baldwin managed to claim one bomber destroyed, but was badly shot up in return and managed to land safely at Sembawang. Pilot Officer 'Jim' Cranstone, who had been separated from his colleagues, gained strikes on another, but could only claim it as damaged as his guns stopped. Then he was chased by three 'Zeros', but managed to take evasive action. Sergeant Fisken claimed one bomber as damaged and a 'Zero' as probably destroyed, a claim that would later be upgraded to a confirmed victory. This was his fifth success in a week, making him the first and only ace flying the RAF Buffalo. The next day, Singapore was again visited by Japanese Navy aircraft. The squadron could only detail a handful of Buffaloes. Sergeant Bert Wipiti, for his third and fourth victories, claimed two G3M bombers shot down, but this was sadly balanced by the loss of 'Ginger' Baldwin, who was killed when his aircraft, W8187/R, was seen to fall into the Straits of Johor, and Sgt Vin Arthur who was killed while flying Fisken's regular mount, W8147/O. By now, 243 was operating with a very small number of aircraft and pilots. On the 23rd, early in the morning, the squadron flew a combined sortie with No. 488 Squadron, three Buffaloes being airborne to patrol over a bridge between Batu Pahat and Kluang. They were caught by Ki-27s and Sgt M.A. Greenslade was shot down, but survived when he baled out very low, his parachute opening just in time. He was back at the squadron for lunch. At the end of the day, 243 had no Buffaloes left serviceable and its sister unit, 488, only had two. However, as 488 was advised it was to be equipped with Hurricanes, its two remaining Buffaloes were handed over to the 243, together with some pilots. The next day, a couple of Buffaloes were dispatched to intercept enemy aircraft reported attacking troops in the Ayer Hitam area. On the way, the pilots encountered a number of twin-engine bombers over the Kluang-Gemas area and P/O Pevreal, in WP-M, damaged two of them while Sgt Kronk in WP-L claimed a third. On the 25th, in the late evening, the weather in the morning was not conducive for ops, 243 provided six aircraft to a mixed force of twelve Buffaloes to strafe transport vehicles beyond Batu Pahat. Some trucks were left burning. Soon after, another patrol was involved in an interception of 27 Army 97 bombers at 15,000 feet during which Sgt Greenslade, in WP-H, claimed one bomber as probably destroyed. The following day, 243 was down to five serviceable Buffaloes, a paltry force considering Japanese landings were imminent. That day, F/L Garden led A Flight to escort a single Vildebeest, while F/L Bertie Bows took B Flight to a point south of Endau to cover the return of the strike force attacking a Japanese fleet spotted by an Australian Hudson. A fierce combat with Japanese fighters took place over the Endau estuary. Flight Lieutenant Garden sealed the fate of a Ki-27 by rolling over on his back and shooting it down while upside down. Garden was then hit by another Japanese fighter, but even though severely damaged, he managed to return his aircraft to Kallang. In the meantime, Sgt Wipiti bagged another Ki-27. On return, Garden was tasked with sending two pilots to strafe the beaches where the Japanese were landing. Pilot Officer Pevreal and Sgt Kronk did the job, protected by Pilot Officers Greenhalgh and Cranstone. The latter reported an engagement with a 'Zero' he claimed as probably destroyed and believed to have crashed in Johor. It was later confirmed. This was the last confirmed victory for 243 while flying the Buffalo. The final victory, but not the final ops. The following day, on the 27th, Sergeants Wipiti and Kronk flew a two-hour reconnaissance and, later in the day, P/O Gifford led B Flight on a recce to report on the enemy shipping bombed the day before. During the day, standard patrols were also flown and P/O Pevreal and Sgt Greenslade found themselves in the middle of an air raid to Kallang. Both managed to escape, but Greenslade's Buffalo was badly shot up. On the ground, damage was considerable with all surviving Buffaloes either destroyed or damaged. Then, while personnel were attempting to salvage aircraft and stores, a second wave of bombers approached. Most of the bombs fell near 243's dispersal, destroying two more Buffaloes. At that time, two Buffaloes were in the air, Pilot Officers Marra and Cranstone, and tried to intercept the Japanese formation, eventually claiming one escorting fighter each. These raids brought the end of 243 Squadron as a unit. Later in the day, orders were received to hand over what they could to the Australians of 453 Squadron, the last Buffalo unit. Over the next few days, some pilots and officers were evacuated and 243 was disbanded before the end of January.

Buffalo AN196/WP-B, almost intact after Singapore surrendered, being inspected by a Japanese soldier.

Date	Pilot	SN	Origin	Type	Serial	Code	Nb	Cat.
13.12.41	Sgt Geoffrey B. **FISKEN**	NZ401556	RNZAF	Ki-48	**W8147**	WP-O	1.0	P
10.01.42	Sgt Charles T. **KRONK**	NZ41514	RNZAF	Ki-46		WP-A	0.50	C
	Sgt Bert S. **WIPITI**	NZ41388	RNZAF				0.50	C
12.01.42	F/L Mombray **GARDEN**	RAF No. 76482	RAF	Ki-27	**W8139**	WP-B	2.0	C
				Ki-27			1.0	P
	F/O Maurice H. **HOLDER**	RAF No. 44070	RAF	Ki-27			2.0	C
	Sgt Geoffrey B. **FISKEN**	NZ401556	RNZAF	Ki-27	**W8147**	WP-O	1.0	C
	P/O Noel C. **SHARP**	NZ411455	RNZAF	Ki-27	**W8138**		1.0	P
	P/O Gordon L. **BONHAM**	NZ402434	RNZAF	G3M		WP-F	1.0	C
				G3M			1.0	P
	Sgt Arthur R. **REYNOLDS**	NZ405819	RNZAF	Ki-27	**W8238**		2.0	P
13.01.42	F/L Mombray **GARDEN**	RAF No. 76482	RAF	Ki-27	**W8242**	WP-K	1.0	C
	P/O Noel C. **SHARP**	NZ411455	RNZAF	Ki-27	**W8138**		1.0	C
	P/O Edgard A. **PEVREAL**	NZ401029	RNZAF	Ki-43	**W8184**	WP-G	0.50	C
	Sgt Charles T. **KRONK**	NZ41514	RNZAF		**W8139**	WP-B	0.50	C
14.01.42	Sgt Geoffrey B. **FISKEN**	NZ401556	RNZAF	A6M	**W8147**	WP-O	1.0	C
15.01.42	P/O Terence B. **MARRA**	NZ403467	RNZAF	Ki-27	**W8143**		1.0	C
	F/L Mombray **GARDEN**	RAF No. 76482	RAF	A6M	**W8242**	WP-K	0.50	C
	Sgt Rex A. **WEBER**	NZ404979	RNZAF		**W8139**	WP-B	0.50	C
16.01.42	S/L Frank J. **HOWELL**	RAF No. 39612	RAF	C5M	**W8193**	WP-V	1.0	C
	Sgt Charles T. **KRONK**	NZ41514	RNZAF	Ki-43		WP-A	1.0	P
17.01.42	F/O Maurice H. **HOLDER**	RAF No. 44070	RAF	Ki-48			1.0	C
							1.0	P
							0.50	C
							0.50	C
	Sgt Geoffrey B. **FISKEN**	NZ401556	RNZAF	Ki-48	**W8147**	WP-O	1.0	C
							0.50	C
							0.50	C
18.01.42	P/O Noel C. **SHARP**	NZ411455	RNZAF	A6M	**W8138**		1.0	C
	Sgt Mervyn J.F. **BALDWIN**	RAF No. 771896	RAF	A6M	**W8187**	WP-R	1.0	C
	Sgt Vincent **ARTHUR**	NZ405519	RNZAF	A6M			1.0	P
	Sgt Charles T. **KRONK**	NZ41514	RNZAF	A6M	**W8242**	WP-K	1.0	P
	P/O Terence B. **MARRA**	NZ403467	RNZAF	*Fighter*	**W8143**		1.0	P
	P/O Edgard A. **PEVREAL**	NZ401029	RNZAF	Ki-48		WP-E	1.0	P
20.01.42	Sgt Charles T. **KRONK**	NZ41514	RNZAF	Ki-48	**W8184**	WP-G	1.0	C
	P/O Noel C. **SHARP**	NZ411455	RNZAF	Ki-48	**W8162**		1.0	C
21.01.42	Sgt Bert S. **WIPITI**	NZ41388	RNZAF	A6M	**W8147**	WP-O	1.0	C
	Sgt Mervyn J.F. **BALDWIN**	RAF No. 771896	RAF	G4M			1.0	C
	Sgt Geoffrey B. **FISKEN**	NZ401556	RNZAF	A6M	**W8147**	WP-O	1.0	C
	Sgt Charles T. **KRONK**	NZ41514	RNZAF	A6M	**W8242**	WP-K	1.0	P
22.01.42	Sgt Bert S. **WIPITI**	NZ41388	RNZAF	G3M			2.0	C
25.01.42	Sgt Maxwell A. **GREENSLADE**	NZ404865	RNZAF	G3M		WP-H	1.0	P
26.01.42	F/L Mombray **GARDEN**	RAF No. 76482	RAF	Ki-27			1.0	C
	Sgt Bert S. **WIPITI**	NZ41388	RNZAF	Ki-27			1.0	C
	P/O James M. **CRANSTONE**	NZ405520	RNZAF	A6M	**W8226**		1.0	C

Total: 24.0

Date	Pilot	S/N	Origin	Serial	Code	Fate
08.12.41	F/O Maurice H. **HOLDER**	RAF No. 44070	RAF	**W8196**		-
03.01.42	Sgt Charles J.P. **POWELL**	NZ404941	RNZAF	**AN197**		Inj.
05.01.42	Sgt Paul L. **ELLIOTT**	NZ402467	RNZAF	**W8199**	WP-S	†
	P/O Ronald S. **SHIELD**	NZ404954	RNZAF	**W8179**		†
12.01.42	Sgt Noel B. **RANKIN**	NZ404942	RNZAF	**W8234**		†
	Sgt Reginald J. **NEWMAN**	NZ41995	RNZAF	**W8137**	WP-C	†
13.01.42	Sgt Arthur R. **REYNOLDS**	NZ405819	RNZAF	**W8238**		†
15.01.42	Sgt John B. **OLIVER**	NZ402888	RNZAF	**W8178**	WP-Y	†
22.01.42	Sgt Mervyn J.F. **BALDWIN**	RAF No. 771896	RAF	**W8187**	WP-R	†
	Sgt Vincent **ARTHUR**	NZ405519	RNZAF	**W8147**	WP-O	†
23.01.42	Sgt Maxwell A. **GREENSLADE**	NZ404865	RNZAF	**W8184**	WP-G	-
27.01.42	*destroyed in air raid*	-	-	**W8155**		-
	destroyed in air raid	-	-	**W8156**		-

Total: 13[1]

[1] Known losses

While the two victors of 10 January 1942 survived the disaster in Singapore, they did not survive the war. Charles Kronk (left) only survived for a few months before being killed in a flying accident on 28 May 1942 while serving with 67 Sqn in India. Bert Wipiti (right), of Maori parentage, lost his life flying a Spitfire with 485 Sqn in Europe on 3 October 1943. He had been awarded the DFM for his actions over Singapore. *(Kronk family left via P. Sortehaug)*

Other pilots who had the opportunity to distinguish themselves over Singapore. Top left: F/L M. Garden, a British pilot, was established and trained at Singapore before the war as a reserve member of the Straits Settlements Volunteer Air Force. When war broke out he was mobilised and in 1941 attended a Buffalo conversion course before being posted as a flight commander. He was evacuated before the fall of the island and returned to the UK where he served until the cessation of hostilities. He received the DFC at the end of the war. Top right, Edgar Pevreal, a New Zealander, was evacuated and remained in India where he served with Nos. 67 and 146 Squadrons and would eventually take command of 17 Sqn in July 1944 (note his initials EAP on the Mae West jacket).

Bottom left: Jim Cranstone, another New Zealander, joined 67 Sqn for a short time after Singapore before being posted to 146 Sqn. He later served with 11 Sqn and was given command of 5 Sqn in 1944. He ended the war with a DFC.

Bottom right: Terry Marra, as with his two previous squadron mates, was evacuated and served with Nos. 67 and 146 Squadrons in India. All survived the war.

(all via P. Sortehaug)

Summary of the aircraft lost by accident - 243 Squadron

Date	Pilot	S/N	Origin	Serial	Code	Fate
08.04.41	P/O Edgard A. **Pevreal**	NZ401029	RNZAF	**W8149**		-
12.05.41	Sgt Alfred R.P. **Saul**	NZ39014	RNZAF	**W8194**		-
22.07.41	P/O Frank W.J. **Oakden**	NZ401028	RNZAF	**W8182**		-
16.08.41	Sgt John B. **Oliver**	NZ402888	RNZAF	**W8134**[1]	WP-M	-
16.11.41	P/O Gordon L. **Bonham**	NZ402434	RNZAF	**W8154**		-
25.11.41	Sgt Alan J. **Lawrence**	NZ402193	RNZAF	**W8189**	WP-Q	-

Total: 6

[1] Final fate uncertain - see photo p17

Victories - confirmed or probable claims: 44.0

First operational sortie:
??.12.41

Last operational sortie:
05.02.42

Number of sorties: ca.500

Total aircraft written-off: 35

Aircraft lost on operations: 26
Aircraft lost in accidents: 9

Squadron code letters:
TD

COMMANDING OFFICERS				
S/L William F. Allshorn	Aus. 165	RAAF	17.07.41	09.10.41
S/L William J. Harper	RAF No. 40110	RAF	09.10.41	...

SQUADRON USAGE

Formed at Bankstown, New South Wales, on 23 May 1941, this was the third Australian fighter squadron raised under the Article XV Agreement. Flight Lieutenant W.K. Wells was appointed as temporary commanding officer and adjutant. It was always intended the squadron would serve overseas and, due to the rising tensions regarding Japanese activities in the Far East during the second half of 1940, the squadron was sent to Malaya to reinforce the Singapore garrison. Nineteen pilots and 145 ground staff

Born in India, William Harper enlisted in the RAF with a short service commission in 1937. With 17 Sqn he saw action over Dunkirk and in the Battle of Britain before being wounded in action on 15 August. He returned to the squadron after recovering before he was posted out as an instructor in March 1941. After this rest period, he was posted to the Far East to take command of 453 Sqn. After being evacuated, he was posted as CO of 135 Sqn in India before being sent to the Middle East where he commanded 92 Sqn between January and May 1943, his last operational posting. His lack of consideration towards his Australian pilots, and his lack of combat activity during his command of 453, led to numerous criticisms after the war. He's seated in his aircraft believed to be AN213/TD-Z

453 Squadron Buffaloes lined up in November 1941. In front (and below) is Buffalo AN185/TD-V flown by 'Doug' Vanderfield, one of the very few pilots who became an ace flying the type. Behind are AN210/TD-J and W8209/TD-E.

Above and below:
The visit by the AOC FE Command, on 19 November 1941, to the two Australian units, Nos. 21 and 453 Squadrons, was highly publicised and many of these photographs were published in a Malayan newspaper at the time. The aim was to show the strength of the Commonwealth forces around Singapore. It seems, however, that it was not enough to convince the Japanese not to invade the Malayan Peninsula.

A Flight, 453 Squadron, posing during the autumn of 1941.
Front, from left to right: Sergeants V.A. Collyer, J. Austin (†25.09.42 while flying a 1 PRU Buffalo in Australia, see later), A.W.B. Clare and M.N. Read (†22.12.41).
Back from left to right: Sergeants K. Gorringe (B Flight), W.R. Halliday, K.R. Leys (B Flight), S/L W.J. Harper, F/L R.D. Vanderfield, Sergeants H.H. Griffiths and S.G. Scrimgeour, and P/O G.L. Angus.

embarked on the steamships *Marella* and *Takoomba* for Singapore in mid-July and the first group arrived at Sembawang on 15 August 1941.

Shortly after the unit arrived at the airfield, a number of Australians, already based there, were posted to the unit to make up for a shortfall in pilots. Squadron Leader W.F. Allshorn, an Australian, took command on 17 August and by the end of the month the squadron had been equipped with Buffaloes and begun training on the aircraft.

It must be said that the underestimation of the capabilities of Japanese aircraft was shared by most of the high-ranking officers in Singapore and political leaders in the United Kingdom, USA and the Netherlands East Indies, all three operators of the Buffalo. The type can be seen as a part of the looming military disaster, but certainly not the cause of it.

Meanwhile, the pilots were flying every day to bring the squadron up to operational readiness as early as possible. Changes in the command structure occurred during those few weeks. Squadron Leader W.F. Allshorn was replaced by a RAF officer, S/L W.J. Harper, in October. He brought with him two Australians, Flight Lieutenants Doug Vanderfield and Mike Grace, as the leaders of A and B Flight respectively. Both had started their tours in England. In three months the unit logged around 1500 hours of flying training with only one man, P/O M. Irvine-Brown, killed on 8 October. Two other Buffaloes were wrecked during the training phase: W8188 on the 12th and W8197 six days later. Both pilots escaped major injury. This was an acceptable loss rate for pilots who had just graduated from training. The squadron was declared operational on 19 November 1941. At that time, 453 had Buffaloes W8151/C, W8152/F, W8157/M, W8158/N, W8159, W8160, W8176, W8180/U, W8188, W8192, W8197, W8202, W8205/H, W8210, W8217/B, W8231/G, AN185/V, AN210/J and AN213/Z on hand.

By now war with Japan appeared imminent and No.2 Degree of Readiness was introduced on 1 December. The unit had 23 pilots ready for action, all but two were Australians. The squadron was temporarily led by an Irish pilot, F/L Tim Vigors RAF, attached from No. 243 Squadron. Pilot Officer D.R.L. Brown, a New Zealander, was the other non-Australian pilot. Tim Vigors replaced Harper who had left for Australia. Harper was not satisfied with the competency of some of his pilots, whom he thought would not perform very well against the Japanese, and he was allowed to try to find some experienced pilots in Australia to reinforce the squadron. A few days later a RAAF Lockheed Hudson observed a Japanese fleet, well south of Indochina, heading in a westerly direction and, on 6 December, No.1 Degree of Readiness was declared. War with Japan was now a matter of hours away.

War came to the Malayan Peninsula on 8 December 1941 (as mentioned earlier, due to time zones, this was before the attack on Pearl Harbor) with the invasion of southern Thailand by the Japanese Army and an air raid on Singapore by Japanese bombers. The squadron was at readiness, with engines warmed up and ready to take off, but they could not obtain orders to intercept the attackers. Surprisingly, the next two days were quiet for the unit, but the pilots had become unsettled and two Buffaloes were lost in accidents. The first was on the 9th when Sgt V.A. Collier had to make an emergency landing after engine failure. In the evening,

Sgt E.A. Peterson was involved in a ground collision with a Dutch Martin 139. A number of these aircraft had arrived at Sembawang under a mutual defence agreement.

Meanwhile Force Z, comprising HMS *Repulse* and HMS *Prince of Wales*, had sailed in search of the Japanese fleet. The squadron was tasked with providing air cover for the ships, which were seen by a Japanese submarine on 9 December and, as they came within range of the Japanese bombers based at Saigon, in French Indochina, an attack was launched against them. As the British ships had changed course, without notifying Singapore, immediate air cover was impossible. The ships were attacked by aircraft on 10 December and both were sunk in a very short time. The squadron took off in response to calls for help, but arrived too late to prevent the disaster. These first few days were frustrating for the pilots who were not able to carry out the job they were trained for. After mounting patrols for the next two days the squadron was ordered north to Ipoh to assist No. 21 Squadron RAAF, the other Australian Buffalo unit, based close to the Thai border. This unit had been in action against the Japanese from the start and its losses of men and equipment were beginning to mount. On 13 December, while en route in three formations, the squadron claimed its first kill. After refueling at Butterworth, F/L R.D. Vanderfield and Sergeants V.A. Collyer and M.N. Read sighted enemy aircraft bombing Penang. They subsequently claimed to have destroyed five of them, Vanderfield making his claims with the undercarriage still unretracted as he was having trouble with it. Read and Collier then successfully strafed enemy troops north of Alor Star. Shortly afterwards another formation of 453's aircraft refueled at Butterworth and, after taking off, were engaged by a large force of enemy aircraft raiding the area. In this combat the unit suffered its first operational casualties. Sergeant R.R. Oelrich was missing, believed killed, and the temporary commanding officer was badly burned in the same action and would not fly again before the end of the campaign. Flight Lieutenant B.A. Grace claimed to have destroyed an enemy fighter. Regrettably, the squadron was to lose another two pilots, and three Buffaloes, before its transfer to Ipoh was complete. The last formation, led by P/O T.W. Livesey, and helped by W/C L.J. Neale (OC Sungai Patani Station), who had offered to ferry a Buffalo due to the lack of pilots, encountered bad weather and tried to make a precautionary landing in a field, but it proved to be unsuitable and disaster occurred. Livesey's aircraft was wrecked as he touched down, but he survived without injury. Neale was killed as was P/O D.R.L. Brown, the only New Zealander serving with the unit. This was the squadron's first contact with the enemy and, with the loss of seven aircraft, three pilots killed, and one severely injured, it was a bloody one. While a Japanese aircraft had fallen to an Australian, the squadron would not survive for long at this rate.

Regardless of the losses, the pilots were sent out the following day to try to stop Japanese forces advancing from the Thai border. Flying with 21 Squadron pilots on a strafing mission, Sergeants G.R. Board and G. Seagoe intercepted some Japanese aircraft. Board claimed a Nakajima Ki-43 shot down while Seagoe claimed another as damaged. The Australians were sent out twice in the afternoon to strafe Japanese positions, but one operation was aborted. On the 15th they were able to intercept a large formation of Kawasaki Ki-48 light bombers and Sergeants M.D. O'Mara and E.A. Peterson shared in the destruction of one bomber, despite half their guns failing. It appears that the problem lay with the poor quality of the weapons carried by the Buffaloes and it was never completely resolved.

An Australian soldier standing in front of one of the squadron's Buffaloes to prevent any acts of sabotage. The aircraft is W8157/TD-M. It would serve until the end before being damaged by enemy shell on 5 February 1942 and not repaired.

In the afternoon, S/L W.J. Harper, who had just returned from Australia, arrived at Ipoh with a few pilots and aircraft to reinforce the squadron. Patrols were flown over the following days in an attempt to have some form of early warning system, but these caused excessive pilot fatigue and consumed the limited number of spares available. Aircraft serviceability dropped rapidly as a result.

During the next few days the Japanese were rarely seen, however, on the 17th, three fighters were intercepted by the Buffaloes, but the result was inconclusive. Meanwhile Japanese bombers dropped their bombs on the airfield facilities and dispersals and destroyed two Buffaloes on the ground. The following day two more Buffaloes were destroyed on the ground and one was destroyed while taking off, but its pilot, Sgt G.R. Board, escaped without injury. It was becoming obvious that the pressure was too great and on the night of 18 December instructions were received to send all serviceable aircraft to Singapore while, at the same time, what remained of 453 Squadron was transferred to Kuala Lumpur. Some reinforcements arrived on the 20th just in time to intercept Japanese raiders the following day. Sergeant Ross Leys was shot down by enemy fighters, but escaped unhurt while Sgt E.A. Peterson claimed one aircraft destroyed and two probables.

On 22 December the first true air battle of the campaign occurred over Kuala Lumpur. The morning started as usual with an airfield defence patrol that lasted two hours and twenty minutes. Soon afterwards, twelve Buffaloes, led by F/L D. Vanderfield, were scrambled to attack a large formation of Japanese bombers and escorts. No less than eleven claims were made that day with four being confirmed. This was probably the Buffalo's biggest success during the whole campaign, but the cost was high with five shot down and three pilots killed. The success was all in vain as the survivors were ordered to return to Sembawang the next day.

The lack of replacement pilots and aircraft obliged RAF Headquarters to merge the two Australian units into one, provisionally known as 21/453 Squadron, under the command of S/L Harper, although most of the operational flights were led by F/L 'Kongo' Kinninmont from 21 Squadron. Until the end of the year the combined unit was tasked with carrying out reconnaissance flights for III Indian Corps, but only a few of these sorties actually took place.

In January 1942, work continued on stripping the Buffalo of excess weight in an endeavour to improve its performance. The wireless masts and rear vision mirrors were removed, gun cowlings flattened, and the size of the gun ports reduced. Verey tubes, parachute flare bins and the cockpit heater were also removed and two 0.50-in wing guns were replaced with 0.303-in guns, reducing the ammunition capacity. The aircraft's weight was reduced by 1000lbs. However, major technical issues continued, including the lack of fuel pressure (the engines were former civilian-rated units). In the new unit structure, 21/453 made its first sorties of the year on 3 January, with six defensive patrols, led by the new CO, over a convoy. This patrol was uneventful even though the unit lost another Buffalo, that flown by Sgt H.H. Griffiths, in an accident. Having lost the formation, he was obliged to make a forced landing 100 miles south-east of Singapore and the Buffalo flipped over. He suffered bad facial injuries in the process. After two days of quiet, 21/453 returned for more convoy patrols while F/L R.A. Kirkman and F/O G.M. Sheppard carried out a tactical reconnaissance of Port Dickson and Dindings on the 6th. When no operational sorties were flown, the squadron was involved in training and various exercises in conjunction with 453 Squadron. Frustrating operations were carried out over the next few days.

On the 9th the squadron attempted an attack on Kuluan, but bad weather prevented this from being pressed home. Of the twelve aircraft dispatched, F/L R.D. Vanderfield struck a soft patch while taxiing and stood his aircraft on its nose as did F/L J.R. Kinninmont, although he was doing about 50mph at the time so his aircraft was considerably bent. Later that day, F/O H.V. Montefiore and Sgt N.R. Chapman made a tactical reconnaissance of the Selangor River, the aircraft refuelling en route at Batu Pahat. The mission was achieved without incident. The following day it was the turn of Sgt G.R. Board to have an accident when his aircraft struck the wing commander's car. Both the car and the Buffalo were damaged beyond repair. On 12 January standing patrols were flown in the morning to intercept possible raids, but the enemy was not encountered. In the beginning of the afternoon, around 14.30, four Buffaloes led by F/L Kirkman took off for an offensive patrol. On the return journey two hours later, F/O R.A. Wallace and Sgt G.T. Harrison (formerly 21 Squadron) collided while weaving. The latter's propeller was knocked off and, as he was too low to bale out, he force-landed W8202 among trees just off Mersing. Harrison was unhurt, but it took him six days to get back. Wallace struggled to keep his damaged AN171 airborne, but when they reached the sea near Tangora, he was forced to ditch, injuring himself in the process. It was a week before Wallace was back in Singapore. While both pilots escaped injury, another two Buffaloes were lost. In four days, five Buffaloes had been lost without inflicting any damage on the Japanese. Convoy patrols were flown the following day. While the enemy aircraft were seen approaching, they did not attack the convoy. On the 14th, one tactical reconnaissance sortie was flown by two ex-21 pilots, F/O D.M. Sproule and Sgt H. Parsons, to Kuantan where thirty Navy 'Zeros' were seen on the ground.

On the 15th, at first light, another tactical reconnaissance was flown by Flying Officers G.M. Sheppard and B. Hood over Seremban and Gemas and a large convoy of motor vehicles was sighted and strafed. Later, bombers returned to bomb Singapore and six Buffaloes, led by Flight Lieutenants Vanderfield and Kinninmont, took off to intercept the raiders, but only three of them reached the enemy aircraft. Two Ki-48s were claimed as destroyed by the two flight lieutenants while P/O F.L. Bowes claimed another as a probable. The day was not yet over for the Australians as in the afternoon a dozen aircraft escorted a mixed formation of RAAF Hudsons, RAF Bristol Blenheims and Dutch Martin 139s to attack a Japanese convoy. The next day F/O Geoff Sheppard claimed a

probable kill on a Japanese reconnaissance aircraft while escorting Dutch Martin 139s and, later in the day, strafing sorties were carried out. On the 17th the Australians were credited with three Japanese fighters claimed by Flight Lieutenants Vanderfield and Grace, and Sgt Clare. The following day it was the turn of F/O D.M. Sproule to shoot down a Nakajima Ki-27 while on a sortie to strafe Japanese motor transport. Later in the day 21/453 Squadron lost another pilot, Sgt N. Chapman, who was shot down and killed by a Ki-43 while escorting RAAF Hudsons. Sergeant H. Parsons claimed a Japanese fighter as probably destroyed. The 18th of January 1942 was a busy day for the Australians who flew reconnaissance flights and then escorted Allied bombers.

The following morning, the 19th, five CAC Wirraways, acting as light bombers, were attacked by Japanese fighters, but the pilots of 21/453 Squadron arrived in time for F/L Bob Kirkman to shoot down a Japanese 'fighter', identified as a "Navy 96" but it was actually a Mitsubishi Ki-51 dive bomber. Two other Ki-51s tried to flee, but were pursued by F/L Vanderfield and Sgt Gorringe who each claimed one aircraft. Japanese fighters soon arrived on the scene and shot down Sgt Henry Parsons. On the flight home some Japanese aircraft, identified as "Navy Os", were observed attacking ground targets. Flight Lieutenant Kirkman attacked one of them and claimed it as a probable. Early in the afternoon five pilots took off for an offensive sweep over Muar and were soon joined by a few Buffaloes from No. 488 (NZ) Squadron. The formation was surprised by Japanese 'Zeros' that shot down two of the New Zealanders. The Australians were luckier and 'Kongo' Kinninmont claimed one fighter. The next few days passed quietly, but on 21 January F/L Kinninmont and Sgt Board collided while escorting Royal Navy Albacores. Although both aircraft returned to base safely, the two Buffaloes could not be repaired in time to defend Singapore during the last battle for the island. At this stage of the campaign the situation was critical and Buffalo spares were becoming increasingly rare. The ground crews did a fantastic job in trying to put every available Buffalo into the air, however a batch of Hurricanes arrived from the United Kingdom and gave the Buffalo pilots some breathing space.

The expected Japanese invasion of Singapore was now very close to becoming a reality. Major changes occurred during the last week of January. The squadron's last hope was a batch of new pilots recently arrived in Singapore. Unfortunately, they were all inexperienced, some having not even completed their training, so, due to a lack of aircraft, it was practically impossible to provide additional training to these pilots. On 26 January, after some days of inactivity, 21/453 Squadron was sent to escort nine RAAF Hudsons to their target, the Japanese landing force. The formation was intercepted by the Japanese and in the furious mêlée that followed, three Australian pilots, F/L B.A. Grace, F/O G.M. Sheppard and Sgt K. Leys, each claimed a Ki-27. Sheppard put the nose of his aircraft down slightly to increase his speed and attacked in a vertical climb, only to have the Ki-27 blow up incredibly close to him. The Buffalo entered a violent spin due to the lack of airspeed, and came out of it after descending 8000 feet, with more Japanese on his tail. Sheppard was fired at several times, but he returned to base to count 126 holes in his aircraft! During the fight

F/O Barrie Hood's Buffalo was badly damaged by Japanese fighters, but he managed to get it back to the airfield.

The following day, news was received that 21 was to return to Australia. Now, with the re-equipment of No. 488 (NZ) Squadron underway, the disbandment of 243 Squadron, and the withdrawal of most of 21 Squadron's pilots to Australia as no aircraft were available, 453 Squadron regained its individual identity and, from that day, was the last Buffalo unit fighting in Singapore. Some Kiwi pilots from both 243 and 488 Squadrons were attached to the Australian unit that then had too many pilots for the few aircraft still capable of being flown. However, morale was high and they were still shooting down Japanese aircraft.

On 29 January Sgt K. Gorringe claimed a bomber as probably destroyed, but had to crash land his Buffalo after his undercarriage was damaged by a Japanese fighter. On the last day of January another Buffalo was put out of action after being fired at by Hurricanes who mistook it for a Japanese fighter. Fortunately, its Kiwi pilot, Sgt C.T. Kronk, was able to make an emergency landing at Tengah and escaped unhurt.

On 1 February 1942 Mitsubishi Ki-21 bombers, escorted by Ki-43 fighters, attacked Sembawang. The Japanese fighters were engaged by six Buffaloes, led by F/L Kinninmont, the only fighter force able to take off that day. Sergeant Seagoe's aircraft was hit and he had to bale out, while Sgt Fisken, a New Zealand pilot, claimed one fighter destroyed, but was wounded in action. A piece of cannon shell bounced off the bakc of his armour plating, hit the side of the plane and went into his hip. In the same action F/L Kinninmont damaged another one fighter. Not much could be achieved with so few serviceable Buffaloes available, but, on the 4th, F/L Kinninmont led three New Zealand sergeants – Fisken, Kronk and Weber – to carry out a reconnaissance flight. They split into pairs and separated. One pair was shot up by Japanese fighters on the way back. Both aircraft returned to Singapore, but Weber's aircraft was severely damaged. Kinninmont and Kronk encountered two Ki-43s and both were claimed as damaged.

The situation was now desperate so, on the 5th, instructions were received to leave Sembawang as it was being regularly shelled by artillery from around Tengah (already evacuated). The defence of the island was nearly at an end and on the 6th all serviceable aircraft were ordered to fly to Palembang on Sumatra while the ground crew waited to be evacuated. During the few next hours most of the remaining members of the squadron were evacuated to Batavia on Java on HMS *Danae* and SS *City of Canterbury*.

A detachment remained on Singapore to destroy facilities before removing the tattered RAAF flag from the flagpole at Sembawang and boarding a small Norwegian ship for the passage to Java. Now without aircraft, 453 Squadron's personnel left Java on 22 February 1942, aboard SS Orcades, and arrived at Adelaide, South Australia, by way of Colombo, on 15 March. The squadron was disbanded that same day.

Claims - 453 Squadron (Confirmed and Probable)

Date	Pilot	SN	Origin	Type	Serial	Code	Nb	Cat.
13.12.41	F/L Richard D. VANDERFIELD	Aus. 402068	RAAF	Ki-48	AN185	TD-V	2.0	C
				Ki-51			1.0	C
	Sgt Malcolm N. READ	Aus. 402952	RAAF	Ki-51	W8209	TD-E	2.5	C
	Sgt Vivian A. COLLYER	Aus. 402935	RAAF	Ki-51	AN180	GA-B	0.5	C
	F/L Bert A. GRACE	Aus. 402053	RAAF	Ki-27	W8159		1.0	C
14.12.41	Sgt Gregory R. BOARD	Aus. 402845	RAAF	Ki-51			1.0	C
15.12.41	Sgt Gregory R. BOARD	Aus. 402845	RAAF	Ki-48			0.5	C
	Sgt Matthew B. O'MARA	Aus. 402876	RAAF				0.5	C
21.12.41	Sgt Eric A. PETERSON	Aus. 402951	RAAF	Ki-51	W8207		1.0	C
				Ki-51			2.0	C
22.12.41	Sgt Alfred W.B. CLARE	Aus. 402769	RAAF	Ki-51			1.0	C
				Ki-51			1.0	P
				Ki-48			1.0	P
	Sgt Malcolm N. READ	Aus. 402952	RAAF	Ki-43	AN175		1.0	C
	Sgt Harold H. GRIFFITHS	Aus. 402348	RAAF	Ki-27	W8231	TD-G	2.0	C
	F/L Richard D. VANDERFIELD	Aus. 402068	RAAF	Ki-27	AN210	TD-J	1.0	P
				Ki-43			1.0	P
	Sgt Keith GORRINGE	Aus. 402859	RAAF	Ki-27			1.0	P
	Sgt Vivian A. COLLYER	Aus. 402935	RAAF	Ki-43	AN180	GA-B	1.0	C
	Sgt Stanley G. SCRIMGEOUR	Aus. 402986	RAAF	Ki-27	W8160		1.0	P
15.01.42	F/L Richard D. VANDERFIELD	Aus. 402068	RAAF	Ki-48		TD-O	1.0	C
	F/L Jack R. KINNINMONT*	Aus. 584	RAAF	Ki-48	W8157	TD-M	1.0	C
	P/O Frederick L. BOWES	Aus. 402846	RAAF	Ki-48			1.0	P
17.01.42	Sgt Alfred W.B. CLARE	Aus. 402769	RAAF	Ki-27			1.0	C
				A6M			0.5	C
	F/L Richard D. VANDERFIELD	Aus. 402068	RAAF	A6M		TD-O	0.5	C
				Ki-27			0.5	C

Date	Pilot	S/N	Origin	Type	Serial	Code		
	F/L Bert A. **Grace**	Aus. 402053	RAAF	Ki-27			0.5	C
18.01.42	F/O Daryl M. **Sproule***	Aus. 250641	RAAF	Ki-27			1.0	C
	Sgt Henry W. **Parsons***	Aus. 407802	RAAF	Ki-43	**AN170**		1.0	P
19.01.42	F/L Jack R. **Kinninmont***	Aus. 584	RAAF	Ki-51	**W8157**	TD-M	1.0	C
				Ki-43			1.0	C
	F/L Robert A. **Kirkman***	Aus. 474	RAAF	Ki-51			1.0	C
				A6M			1.0	P
	F/L Richard D. **Vanderfield**	Aus. 402068	RAAF	Ki-51			1.0	C
	Sgt Keith **Gorringe**	Aus. 402859	RAAF	Ki-51			1.0	C
26.01.42	F/L Bert A. **Grace**	Aus. 402053	RAAF	Ki-27			1.0	C
	F/O Geoffrey M. **Sheppard**	Aus. 280628	RAAF	Ki-27			1.0	C
	Sgt Keith R. **Leys**	Aus. 402955	RAAF	Ki-27			1.0	C
29.01.42	Sgt Keith **Gorringe**	Aus. 402859	RAAF	G3M			1.0	P
01.02.42	Sgt Geoffrey B. **Fisken**	NZ401556	RNZAF	Ki-43	**W8237**		1.0	C
				A6M			1.0	P

Total: 44.0

* No. 21 Sqn pilot

Summary of the aircraft lost on Operations - 453 Squadron

Date	Pilot	S/N	Origin	Serial	Code	Fate
09.12.41	Sgt Vivian A. **Collyer**	Aus. 402935	RAAF	**W8151**	TD-C	-
	Sgt Eric A. **Peterson**	Aus. 402951	RAAF	**W8210**		-
13.12.41	F/L Timothy A. **Vigors**	RAF No. 33554	(Ire)/RAF	**AN213**	TD-Z	**Inj.**
	P/O Geoffrey L. **Angus**	Aus. 403009	RAAF	**W8152**	TD-F	-
	Sgt Ronald R. **Oelrich**	Aus. 402875	RAAF	**W8225**		†
	Sgt Matthew B. **O'Mara**	Aus. 402876	RAAF	**W8192**		-
	P/O Frederick L. **Bowes**	Aus. 402846	RAAF	**W8217**	TD-B	-
18.12.41	Sgt Gregory R. **Board**	Aus. 402845	RAAF	**W8216**		-
	Sgt Vivian A. **Collyer**	Aus. 402935	RAAF	**W8211**		-
21.12.41	Sgt Keith R. **Leys**	Aus. 402955	RAAF	**W8206**		-
22.12.41	P/O Robert W. **Drury**	Aus. 207698	RAAF	**AN204**		†
	Sgt Malcolm N. **Read**	Aus. 402952	RAAF	**AN175**		†
	Sgt Stanley G. **Scrimgeour**	Aus. 402986	RAAF	**W8160**		-
	Sgt Eric A. **Peterson**	Aus. 402951	RAAF	**W8207**		†
	P/O Thomas W. **Livesey**	Aus. 402870	RAAF	**AN184**		-
03.01.42	Sgt Harold H. **Griffiths**	Aus. 402348	RAAF	**AN211**		-
12.01.42	F/O Granton T. **Harrison***	Aus. 407578	RAAF	**W8202**		-
17.01.42	*Destroyed in air raid*	-	-	**AN173**		-
	Destroyed in air raid	-	-	**AN215**		-
18.01.42	Sgt Norman R. **Chapman***	Aus. 401102	RAAF	**AN174**		†
19.01.42	Sgt Henry W. **Parsons***	Aus. 407802	RAAF	**AN170**		†
27.01.42	*Destroyed in air raid*	-	-	**W8156**		-
29.01.42	Sgt Keith **Gorringe**	Aus. 402859	RAAF	**?**		-
30.01.42	Sgt Matthew B. **O'Mara**	Aus. 402876	RAAF	**AN205**		-
31.01.42	Sgt Charles T. **Kronk**	NZ41514	RNZAF	**W8226**		-
05.02.42	P/O Frank S. **Johnstone**	NZ41335	RNZAF	**W8157**	TD-M	-

Total: 26

* No. 21 Sqn pilot

33

High-ranking officers inspect the damage caused to a Buffalo after a dogfight with Japanese fighters. It is believed that the Buffalo was AN189/TD-C. If so, the pilot involved was Sgt 'Wild Bill' Collyer whose aircraft was damaged in action on 22 December 1941.

Summary of the aircraft lost by accident - 453 Squadron

Date	Pilot	S/N	Origin	Serial	Code	Fate
12.09.41	Sgt Alfred W.B. CLARE	Aus. 402769	RAAF	W8188		-
18.09.41	Sgt Harold H. GRIFFITHS	Aus. 402348	RAAF	W8197		-
18.10.41	P/O Maxwell IRVINE-BROWN	Aus. 404736	RAAF	W8208		†
13.12.41	P/O David R.L. BROWN	NZ41687	RNZAF	W8158	TD-N	†
	W/C Leonard J. NEALE	RAF No. 29174	RAF	W8176		†
	P/O Thomas W. LIVESEY	Aus. 402870	RAAF	W8180	TD-U	-
09.01.42	F/L Richard D. VANDERFIELD	Aus. 402068	RAAF	AN185	TD-V	-
	F/L Jack R. KINNINMONT	Aus. 584	RAAF	W8209		-
10.01.42	Sgt Gregory R. BOARD	Aus. 402845	RAAF	W8219		-

Total: 9

Above: Buffalo W8180/TD-U seen in November 1941 during the display (see the photos p25). It was to be lost less than three weeks later when it crashed and overturned several times in a paddy field after becoming lost due to very bad weather on 13 December. The pilot, P/O T.W. Livesey, was unhurt.

Left: A pre-war misfortune that befell what seems to be W8219/TD-Y. The Buffalo ended up on its nose, but was soon returned to service. It was lost on 10 January 1942 when it taxied into a car at Kluang.

Victories - confirmed or probable claims: 18.0

First operational sortie:
10.10.41
Last operational sortie:
23.01.42

Number of sorties: ca.300

Total aircraft written-off: 19

Aircraft lost on operations: 15
Aircraft lost in accidents: 4

Squadron code letters:
NF

COMMANDING OFFICERS

S/L Wilfred G. CLOUSTON	RAF No. 39223	(NZ)/RAF	10.10.41	23.01.42
S/L John N. MACKENZIE	RAF No. 40547	(NZ)/RAF	23.01.42	...

SQUADRON USAGE

The last unit to be equipped with the Brewster Buffalo was 488 (NZ) Squadron when it was officially formed on 1 September 1941 at Rongotai in New Zealand. It arrived in Singapore (Kallang) in October. Command of the squadron was given to S/L Wilf Clouston, a New Zealander, former Battle of Britain veteran and DFC recipient. He was assisted by two flight commanders who had also fought during the summer of 1940: Flight Lieutenants J.N. Mackenzie DFC and J.R. Hutcheson.

They first received the Buffaloes left behind when 67 Squadron departed for Burma: W8135, W8138/O, W8141, W8148/J, W8150/I, W8153, W8168/T, W8171, W8173, W8174, W8175, W8177, W8183, W8185/V, W8186/X, W8191/D, W8195, W8198/U, W8200, W8223, W8235 and AN198.

Conversion and training started on the 20th, the pilots flying every day. Three Buffaloes were damaged by the end of the month: W8223 and W9198 on the 28th, and W8200 the day after. All the aircraft were repaired and the pilots escaped injury. In November, training continued, but two Buffaloes were wrecked, both on the 14th. W8153 hit a concrete parapet on landing, the pilot, F/T Hutcheson, was unhurt and, ten days later, Sgt E.E.G. Khun survived a crash landing in AN198.

Training continued until the declaration of a state of emergency on 7 December, an attack by Japan imminent. The next day, a state of war existed and at 07.41 two sections were scrambled to fly defensive patrols over the aerodrome. Further patrols were flown at 13.15 and 15.00, but the Japanese did not appear. No ops were carried out on the 9th, but intensive training and gunnery was undertaken as it was not felt the unit was entirely ready for combat. The next day training flights were flown and, in the afternoon, eighteen sorties were carried out with patrols off Tioman Island to escort naval units. The enemy was not seen. During the day the squadron also received ground crew reinforcements from RAF Kallang. During the rest of the month, 488

Initial command of 488 Sqn was given to S/L W.G. Clouston. A New Zealander, he had already been a flight commander with 19 Sqn when war broke out and for his actions over Dunkirk was awarded the DFC in June 1940 before participating in the Battle of Britain. He led 258 Sqn before being sent to Singapore. He led 488 Sqn until being posted to HQ RAF Singapore on 23 January 1942. He was eventually captured on 15 February 1942 and would spend the rest of the war as a PoW. He survived the very harsh conditions of detention and returned to active duty, serving until 1957.

A group photo featuring 488 Sqn in front of their flight hut. Left to right: the two flight leaders, Flight Lieutenants J.N. Mackenzie and J.R. Hutcheson, Sergeants T.W. Honan and H.J. Meharry, Pilot Officers J.C. Godsiff, G.S. Johnstone and E.W. Cox (†18.01.42), Sergeants E.E.G. Kuhn and V.E. Meaclem, Pilot Officers G.P. White, H.S. Pettit and W.J. Greenhalgh, Sergeants P.E.E. Killick, J.F. Burton (†01.07.43 with 14 Sqn RNZAF), D.L. Clow, and C.D. Charters (PoW 19.01.42), and Pilot Officers L.R. Farr (†22.01.42) and P.D. Gifford (squatting with hand in puddle). *(WJ Greenhalgh via P. Sortehaug).*

continued its training and operational flights, but no Japanese aircraft were encountered. However, on 18 December, returning from a patrol, Sgt A.G. Craig, in W8175, was on approach to land back at 15.37 when he was blinded by the sun. Flying too low, the starboard wing of the aircraft collided with trees causing the fighter to crash and burst into flames. The following day sixteen Buffaloes attempted to intercept a Japanese reconnaissance aircraft, but, as with the following day, their efforts were in vain. Ten days later, Buffalo W8200, flown by Sgt W.R. De Maus, collided with a Tiger Moth, of A Flight of the Malayan Volunteer Air Force, over Singapore. The Tiger crashed into Lavender Street, killing the pair on board, which included New Zealander P/O W.W.G. Felton. The month ended with great frustration for the New Zealanders who were unable to engage the enemy. During the month, 488 flew about 200 sorties, and if the two attempts to intercept enemy aircraft are ignored, all sorties consisted of patrols.

The first ten days of January 1942 resembled December, with numerous uneventful patrols flown. On the 3rd the squadron was involved in an incoming convoy escort with the other squadrons. The convoy was transporting reinforcements. The squadron was the first to start the patrols from 07.00, handing over the task to 453 Squadron at the end of the morning. The next day, 488 lost Buffalo W8223 in a landing accident. Its pilot, P/O Jack Godsiff, survived, but was slightly injured. Five days later, Sgt Eddie Kuhn, in W8150/I, narrowly missed opening the unit's score in the afternoon when he sighted a single-engine aircraft and gave chase. As he closed the range, the Japanese reconnaissance aircraft dived into cloud and escaped. The big day would come on the 12th. Early in the morning, no less than 72 Ki-27 fighters appeared above Singapore. In a rather piecemeal effort, eight Buffaloes of A Flight took off to intercept. They were followed by B Flight 26 minutes later. The first section, led by F/L MacKenzie, saw thirty enemy fighters, about 3000 feet above, as the Japanese dived on them. Sergeant Terry Honan's W8200 was hit in the engine almost immediately. It caught fire and Honan baled out to safety at 12,000 feet with a bullet in his left arm. He was soon followed by Sgt Rod MacMillan's W8186/X that fell out of control with most of its tail shot away. MacMillan baled out and landed close to Honan's position. Meanwhile, combat continued and Sgt Jim MacIntosh claimed a Ki-27 as a probable, even though he saw it going into the jungle. With the difficult situation on the ground, it could not be confirmed. Two other Buffaloes escaped after a bad time against the Japanese. Pilot Officer Jack McAneny, in W8150/I, had to make a forced landing and P/O 'Snow' White landed his badly damaged aircraft (W8191/D). Three others were also damaged, but quickly repaired. Arriving too late, B Flight failed to see any action but W8135 flown by Sgt Vern Meaclem, suffered an oil pipe fracture and crash landed near Seletar, the aircraft being a total write-off although without injuries to the pilot.

The next day, the 13th, another raid took place with 81 Japanese bombers, thirty of them (Mitsubishi G3Ms) being intercepted by eight Buffaloes from the squadron. The Kiwis attacked from behind and below, but F/L Hutcheson's Buffalo (W8148/J) was soon hit by return fire. He had to break off and make a forced landing at Tengah. He wasn't the only one, as P/O Jack Oakden was also hit and shot down in W8185/V. He ditched into the sea, but was rescued by fishermen. Sergeant D.L. Clow, in W8235, was also unlucky that day, being another victim of the Japanese rear gunners, and baled out over the sea. He managed to reach land where he was saved by a Dutch party the following day. The Kiwis got their revenge when P/O Wally Greenhalgh (W8168/T), with only two of his guns firing, attacked a bomber and saw smoke issue from one of its engines. In two days, the squadron had lost seven aircraft, with others damaged, for very little success. Bad luck continued to dog the New Zealanders as, the same day, Sgt E.E.G. Kuhn had to bale out of AN187 over the sea when the engine seized and caught fire. The Buffalo was a replacement aircraft and Kuhn was conducting an air test before using it on operations. This machine had been transferred from 243 Squadron to compensate for a 488 pilot, Noel Sharp, who had been attached, with his aircraft, to 243. On the 14th, 488 Squadron, with 243 Squadron, was scrambled to meet 51 Japanese bombers that were turning back before reaching their target due to bad weather. No combat took place. However, the day would prove fruitful for 488 as Sgt Perce Killick, while patrolling with a section, intercepted a reconnaissance aircraft that was claimed as probably destroyed because its escorting 'Zero' forced the Buffalo to break off. On the next day, the 15th, an incoming raid was intercepted at about 10.00. The escort did its job and shot down one of the squadron's aircraft, W8183, flown by P/O G.L. Hesketh. Formerly a 243 Squadron pilot, Hesketh was severely wounded, but managed to crash-land his aircraft on a narrow strip by the oil tanks alongside Alexandra Hospital. However, he was dead by the time ground personnel reached the wrecked machine. On the other hand, two Ki-27s were claimed as shot down, one by Sgt Kuhn and the other one shared by three other pilots. Kuhn's Buffalo was, however, badly damaged, and many others returned with various degrees of damage. The next day, with aircraft strength considerably diminished, the squadron took off to intercept another raid with all available aircraft, but failed to gain sufficient height to carry out an attack. The battle over Singapore was intensifying and the Japanese were sending raids as landings took place. On the 17th, 488 was in action again and P/O P.D. Gifford claimed a Ki-27 as damaged while flying W8173. The Kiwis, though, lost another Buffalo, W8195, from which P/O F.S. Johnstone had to bale out after an engine failure following a full throttle climb and a subsequent loss of oil. It was the third Buffalo lost in the same way within a week. Continuing their harassing raids, the Japanese were over Singapore again on the 18th and 243 and 488 tried to intercept them. The Buffaloes were able to surprise the Japanese and, in the ensuing melee, 488 claimed seven aircraft destroyed or probably destroyed. Sergeants Kuhn and MacIntosh claimed two each. However, it was not a one-sided engagement. Flight Lieutenant Hutcheson was shot down in W8177, crash landing on the shore, but was able to return to the squadron soon afterwards. Pilot Officer E.W. Cox was last seen diving into a cloud over the Singapore Strait and was presumed killed. These victories were the last claimed on the Buffalo by 488. The next day, at 13.40, four Buffaloes from the squadron were seconded to 243 Squadron and headed north along the western Malayan coast to strafe ground targets a mile north of Muar township. Fifty minutes or so later, en route near Batu Pahat, enemy fighters were sighted below. However, as the Buffaloes dived to intercept, they were attacked from above and two were shot down, one of them being flown by P/O K.J. McAneny. Although he was seen to crash, he was lost without trace. The second Buffalo was

Three-fourths front view of a Buffalo of 488 Sqn coded NF-O. The serial is illegible, but is part of the W sequence. It is probaly W8138 as the photo was taken at the end of the monsoon.

38

The same aircraft NF-O with now a personal artwork painted on the cowling. Buffalo Mk.I W8138 was the personal mount of New Zealander P/O Noel Sharp of 488 Sqn.

piloted by Sgt C.D. Charters who managed to baled out only to be captured by the Japanese. Later transported to Thailand, he died there of dysentery on Christmas Day 1943. On the 20th, what remained of 488 and 243 Squadrons scrambled once more, but, having taken off too late, failed to intercept the raid. From that point, 488 Squadron was not able to play a major role due to the heavy losses sustained since the beginning of the month. Only a few sorties could be carried out, generally with 243 Squadron in the lead, and these consisted of Army support or fighter interceptions, the role changing from day to day or even hour to hour! Despite the low number of sorties, 488 lost one last Buffalo on 22 January. That day, around 11.20, Singapore was again raided, this time by 25 G3Ms, with escort fighters, which attacked Kallang as four Buffaloes of 488, almost the entire fighter force of the squadron, were taxiing out. Three got off, but W8191/D was blown into a petrol dump adjacent to the airfield boundary. Its pilot, P/O L.R. Farr, was badly wounded by shrapnel and died three days later. The attack also cost the lives of two crewmen of the squadron, one from the RAF and one from the RNZAF, when they were killed shortly after having started the aircraft. Two Buffaloes were also damaged beyond repair on the ground (W8174 and W8198). The following day, the squadron could only send a handful of aircraft, led by F/L Mackenzie, to patrol over a bridge between Batu Pahat and Kluang to enable retreating soldiers and transport to get across with minimal interference. They were caught by Japanese fighters, but no losses were recorded by 488. By the end of the day, with so few Buffaloes available to both units, particularly for the Kiwis, it was decided to allocate nine recently arrived Hurricanes, four collected immediately, with the remainder following over the next two days. The squadron continued the fight with the Hurricanes until the end of March 1942. The Buffalo era for 488 ended at that time following a short campaign that saw the unit's strength largely wiped out in a couple of combats over two weeks. It is difficult to figure out the number of sorties carried out by the Buffaloes, as all documents were lost for January onwards, but considering a number of factors, about 100 sorties were flown until 22 January, for a total of 300 sorties in about six weeks of operations.

Above: Buffalo W8168/NF-T undergoing repairs before the Japanese invasion. It was later damaged in combat on 20 January 1942, P/O F.W.J. Oakden being unhurt. What happened to it is unknown. However, knowing that spares and time were lacking at the end of January 1942, it is possible that it was never repaired or flown again. *(JE Burton via P. Sortehaug)*
Below: Buffalo W8198/NF-U was destroyed by bomb splinters at Kallang on 22 January 1942.

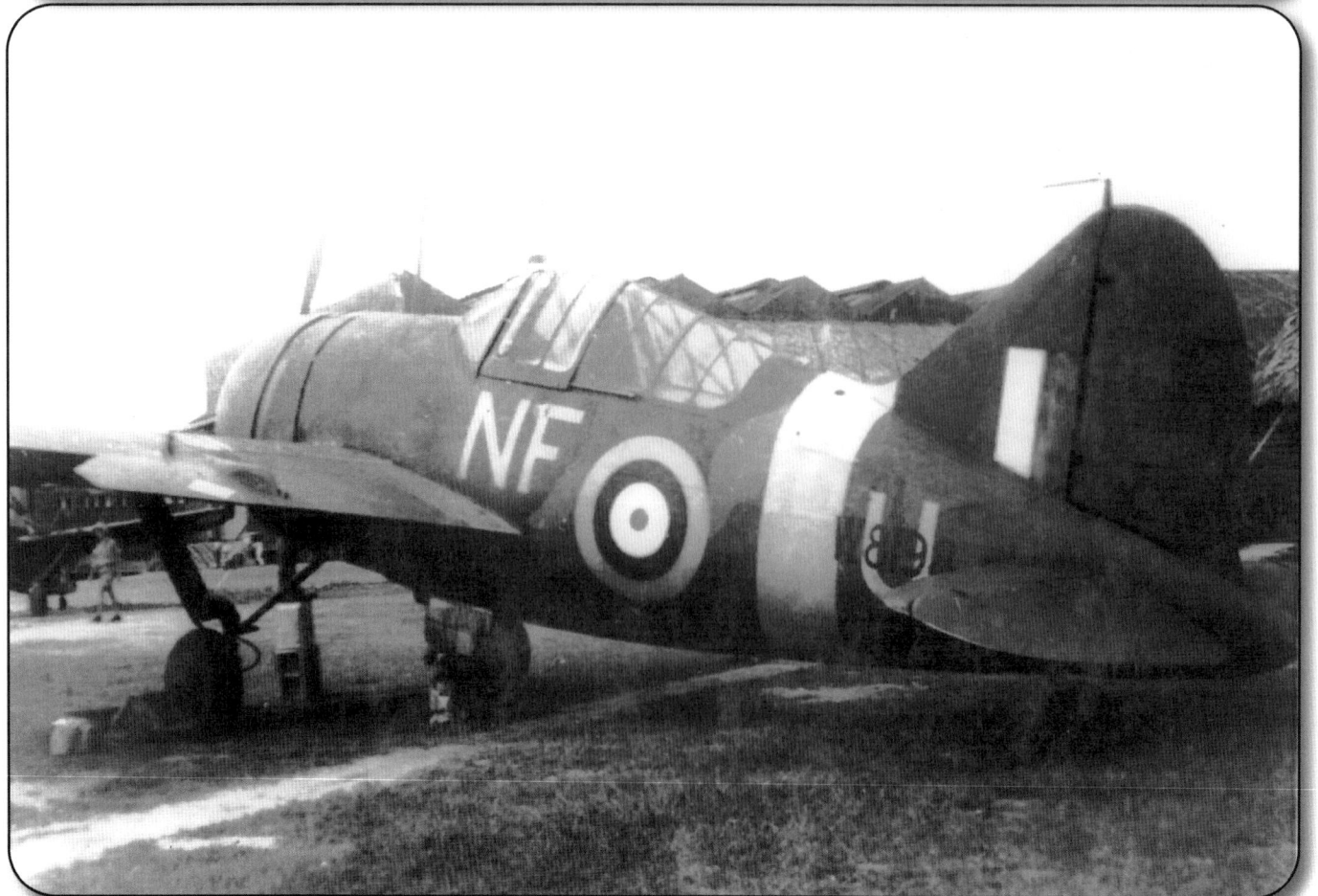

Claims - 488 Squadron (Confirmed and Probable)

Date	Pilot	SN	Origin	Type	Serial	Code	Nb	Cat.
12.01.42	Sgt William J.M. MacIntosh	NZ405297	RNZAF	Ki-27	**W8171**		1.0	P
13.01.42	P/O Walter J. Greenhalgh	NZ41984	RNZAF	G3M	**W8168**	NF-T	1.0	P
14.01.42	Sgt Percy E.E. Killick	NZ41909	RNZAF	Ki-46			1.0	P
15.01.42	Sgt Edmund E.G. Kuhn	NZ41912	RNZAF	Ki-27			1.0	C
	Sgt Donald L. Clow	NZ41877	RNZAF	Ki-27	**W8235**		0.33	C
	Sgt William J.M. MacIntosh	NZ405297	RNZAF		**W8171**		0.33	C
	Sgt Henry J. Meharry	NZ41992	RNZAF				0.33	C
18.01.42	Sgt Edmund E.G. Kuhn	NZ41912	RNZAF	A6M			2.0	C
	Sgt Percy E.E. Killick	NZ41909	RNZAF	A6M			1.0	C
	F/L John R. Hutcheson	NZ39967	RNZAF	A6M	**W8177**		1.0	C
	Sgt Vernon E. Meaclem	NZ41923	RNZAF	A6M	**W8158**		1.0	P
	Sgt William J.M. MacIntosh	NZ405297	RNZAF	A6M	**W8198**	NF-U	2.0	P

Total: 18.0

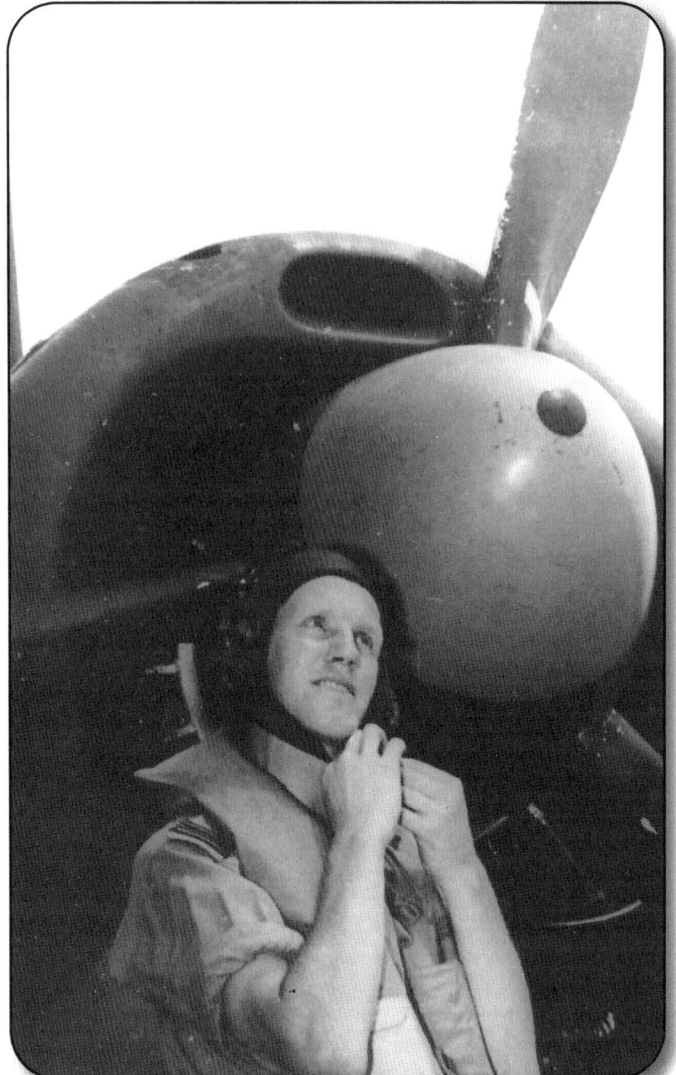

The two 488 Sqn flight commanders. Right: J.N. Mackenzie, A Flight CO, also became the second CO of 488. A New Zealander, he was already a very experienced pilot, having joined the RAF in 1937 on a short service commission. He served the first months of the war with 41 Sqn and made all of his claims (six confirmed victories, four probables and two aircraft damaged) in 1940. He received the DFC in November 1940 and arrived in Singapore in September 1941 to take over A Flight. He eventually led 488 from end January 1942. Later in the war, he was given command of 14 Sqn in the Pacific and 64 Sqn, flying Mustangs over Europe, in 1944. He survived the war and continued to serve in the RAF until 1957. *(J.N. MacIntosh via P. Sortehaug)*

Above: the B Flight CO, F/L J.R.R. Hutcheson. Upon his return to New Zealand, he was with 14 Sqn when it formed in April 1942 as many of the unit's air and ground personnel were 488 Sqn survivors. Hutcheson was medically categorised as unfit for tropical service and consequently did not go with the unit when it left for the Solomon Islands the following year. He became an instructor. *(J.R. Hutcheson via P. Sortehaug)*

Date	Pilot	S/N	Origin	Serial	Code	Fate
18.12.41	Sgt Alexander G. CRAIG	NZ41882	RNZAF	W8175		†
12.01.42	Sgt Roderick W. MACMILLAN	NZ404914	RNZAF	W8166		-
	Sgt Terence W. HONAN	NZ402520	RNZAF	W8200		-
	Sgt Vernon E. MEACLEM	NZ41923	RNZAF	W8135		-
13.01.42	P/O Frank W.J. OAKDEN	NZ401028	RNZAF	W8185	NF-V	-
	Sgt Donald L. CLOW	NZ41877	RNZAF	W8235		-
15.01.42	P/O Greville L. HESKETH	NZ402868	RNZAF	W8183		†
17.01.42	P/O Frank S. JOHNSTONE	NZ41335	RNZAF	W8195		-
18.01.42	F/L John R. HUTCHESON	NZ39967	RNZAF	W8177		-
	P/O Ernest W. COX	NZ41881	RNZAF	W8141		†
19.01.42	P/O Kenneth J. MCANENY	NZ411421	RNZAF	W8171		†
	Sgt Cecil F. CHARTERS [1]	NZ41876	RNZAF	AN189		PoW
22.01.42	P/O Leonard R. FARR [2]	NZ411390	RNZAF	W8191	NF-D	†
	Destroyed in air raid	-	-	W8198	NF-U	-
	Destroyed in air raid	-	-	W8174		-

Total: 15

[1] Died as a PoW 25.12.43
[2] Died of wounds 25.01.42

Sergeant W.J.N. MacIntosh converted to Hurricanes and eventually continued the flight towards Java with Nos. 488 and 605 Squadrons where he was captured in March 1942. He survived captivity.
(via P. Sortehaug)

Date	Pilot	S/N	Origin	Serial	Code	Fate
14.11.41	F/L John R. HUTCHESON	NZ39967	RNZAF	W8153		-
24.11.41	Sgt Edmund E.G. KUHN	NZ41912	RNZAF	AN198		-
04.01.42	P/O John C. GODSIFF	NZ41895	RNZAF	W8223		-
13.01.42	Sgt Edmund E.G. KUHN	NZ41912	RNZAF	AN187		-

Total: 4

Two of 488 Squadron's pilots posing in front of a Buffalo. Above is P/O L.R. Farr in front of his W9181/NF-D. On 22 January, flying this aircraft, he took off with two others, but was hit by shrapnel. He managed to get airborne, but could not maintain control, either because of damage to the aircraft or his own injuries. The Buffalo was seen to dip and rip off the undercarriage before ploughing through a house and the petrol dump building. Farr was found alive in the Buffalo, but died of his wounds three days later.

Below: Sgt V.E. Meaclem in front of W8148/NF-J. He survived the war after being evacuated to New Zealand. As with many other 488 Sqn veterans, he was posted to the newly formed 14 Sqn. *(V.E. Meaclem via P. Sortehaug)*

Buffalo aircraft of 488 Sqdn dispersed at Kallang before the Japanese attack. *(V E Meaclem via P. Sortehaug)*

No. 60 Squadron

The batch of Buffaloes sent to Burma allowed for the formation of a unit at Mingaladon. A C Flight was formed within No. 60 Squadron (Bristol Blenheims) in July 1941. They were to be assembled on the station, but the lack of facilities obliged the squadron to move five Blenheims to storage at Toungoo. The first Buffalo was ready to be flight tested on 29 July, but it flew the next day. From 6 August onwards, the first Buffaloes (AN190, followed by AN191 and AN192 on the 9th and AN193 on the 12th) were delivered to C Flight 60 Squadron. The aircraft suffered hydraulic trouble that led to the grounding of the type on the 21st. All hands were busy putting the Buffaloes back together so little flying was done, just 23 hours for August. Six pilots were converted to the type after initial flying on a Curtiss Falcon of the BVAF. By 31 August, ten Buffaloes had been assembled. This figure had increased to sixteen when the aircraft were handed over to 67 Squadron on arrival from Singapore.

The survivors

The two Buffaloes that had been sent to the UK for various tests, W8132 and W8133, immediately became surplus to RAF requirements with the type being withdrawn from use. The former went in to storage at 5 MU on 5 March and W8133 followed on 1 April. It was decided to use both as instructional airframes on 20 June and they were eventually struck off charge on 17 September 1943 and scrapped.

For the few aircraft that survived the retreat from Burma, their general condition was so poor that no future long-term usage could be considered since the lack of parts would soon become an issue. As a temporary measure, three aircraft (W8246, W8250 and AN214) were used to train pilots from No. 146 Squadron between March and May 1942. The experience was short lived as two of the aircraft, W8246 and AN214, were lost in separate accidents within a month. Buffalo W8246 was lost on 9 April after its brakes failed on landing at Dinjan and AN214 followed suit when the CO, S/L Czernin, and F/L I.L.B. Aitkens, flying An214, were escorting an Audax to Dum Dum. The Buffalo was damaged on landing at Jessore. With no spare parts available for repairs, both aircraft were soon struck off charge. For some reason, at least two aircraft, W8243 and W8245, are often reported to have been used by No. 151 OTU (ex-1 OTU, renamed 151 OTU in July 1942) at Risalpur, but no trace of them can be found in the unit's ORB, consisting of the records of the three flights: Mohawk, Hurricane and Harvard. The monthly flight reports mentioned no hours flown on any Buffalo (if ever they were really assigned to the unit) for the entire year of 1942. Because of the lack of spare parts, they probably saw little use, perhaps as hacks or staff aircraft. The two Buffaloes, in any case, became instructional airframes sometime in 1943 and both, with W8250 (which was probably also issued to 151 OTU), were officially struck off charge in November 1943.

No. 4 PRU

This short-lived unit came to light just before the Japanese attack. It was formed from a request from the Air HQ for a few long-range aircraft for reconnaissance work that went so far unfulfilled. It was therefore decided to equip two Buffaloes drawn from the fighter reserves for this task. As the Brewster F2A had been built for a such purpose, the modifications didn't need a lot of work. The selected aircraft (W8136 and W8166) were stripped of guns and armour plate and a single F.24 camera was installed sighting simply through a download observation window in the cockpit floor but W8166 was also fitted with additional fuel tanks to allow four hours duration giving an additional radius of 700 miles and two more F.24 cameras. The command of this unit was given to Squadron Leader C.R.G. Lewis, an Air HQ's Chief Photographic Officer, soon joined by two other pilots, Flight Lieutenant A D. Philipps from 4 AACU and Sergeant C.B. Wareham posted from 243 Squadron. Many sorties were flown by those three pilots sometimes in perilious conditions and the aircraft survived almost until the end. Sergeant Wareham was also credited with a Japanese fighter destroyed when, while returning from a PR mission, one of his pursuer hit a small hill while flying very low and crashed into it. Buffalo W8136 tried to be evacuated to Bandoeng on 7 February but crashed on landing that day, the pilot, S/L Lewis being slightly injured. The day before, W8166 had been destroyed by shelling at Kallang.

Sergeant Charlie Wareham, a New Zealander, was a former 243 Sqn pilot who was posted to 4 PRU where he flew 32 reconnaissance sorties during the campaign. He was awarded the DFM in March 1942. He continued to serve in India, flying Mohawks with 155 Sqn for a while before returning to PR duty with 681 Sqn and its Hurricanes. He finally returned to New Zealand at the end of 1943. (C.B. Wareham via P. Sortehaug)

WITH THE RAAF

No. 21 Squadron RAAF (code GA)

This Australian squadron arrived in Malaya in September 1940, although it was not yet a fighter squadron. It had flown Wirraways to date, acting as an OTU for fighter squadrons, and was commanded by S/L E.G. Fyfe. Its role in case of war was to use the Wirraways against ships, a role far from satisfactory for the type. However, at the end of the summer of 1941, the threat from the Empire of Japan intensified and the Australian Government became more concerned with the use of 21 Squadron and asked for it to re-equipped with Buffaloes. In August, the FEAF had enough Buffaloes on hand to convert the squadron to the type, even though this was regarded as a temporary measure. The first Buffaloes arrived on the 26th. More aircraft were expected within a week, to bring the allocation to twelve, a bit less than the usual allocation for a fighter squadron. Training began, but attrition soon took its toll when, on 26 September, F/O R.H. Wallace's aircraft, W8214, suffered an engine fire in flight. Wallace abandoned the aircraft and made a nice landing 100 yards from the shore of the Strait of Johor. Uninjured, he was rescued by a boat. In October, the Wirraways left and S/L Allshorn arrived on the 10th to take command, effective from the 13th. That month, the allocation was increased to sixteen Buffaloes, still two under the normal strength. The final aircraft arrived at the end of November despite the squadron being declared operational on the 19th. At the end of November, 21 moved from Sembawang to Sungei Petani on the 25th. Their role was to support the Army. The situation at the aerodrome was poor due to the rainy season in northern Malaya. Furthermore, there was no accommodation for the aircraft and all maintenance had to be performed in the open. As a result, serviceability rates were low and this was compounded by the difficulties experienced in maintaining the Buffaloes specifically, particularly with regard to armament and the hydraulic system. The machine guns were affected by corrosion and components of the electrical system were prone to rust in the wet and humid conditions. The undercarriage gave frequent trouble by jamming in the locked position and even the manual release was not effective in solving the problem.

William F. Allshorn was a regular RAAF officer and was posted to 21 Sqn to take command as it was converting to the Buffalo. When the unit merged with 453 Sqn, he was posted to Singapore in a non-flying position. He managed to evacuate and reached Australia. He started a second tour of operations in December 1942 at the head of 4 Sqn and later served with HQ 78 Wing RAAF.

At 01.30 hours, on 8 December (due to time zones, this was before the attack on Pearl Harbor), 21 RAAF received information that the Japanese had bombed Singapore and had attempted a landing at Kota Bharu. The squadron was called out immediately and arrangements were made to bring all serviceable aircraft to stand-by from first light. Two enemy aircraft were reported approaching from the west at 07.20 hours. Two sections, of two aircraft each, were ordered to await further instructions from the operations room. Ten minutes later, without further warning, a formation of five Ki-27s was seen heading for Sungai Petani at about 11,000 feet. No orders to scramble and intercept were received. The Japanese made their attacks on the aerodrome, destroying two Buffaloes on the ground while two more were damaged by shrapnel, and another two by fire. However, two pilots managed to take off despite the lack of orders. Flight Lieutenant Kirkman and F/O Hooper got airborne, but they failed to reach the fighters. Even if they had, their guns were not working as nothing happened, when both pilots tried to charge their weapons, due to missing solenoids. Patrols were carried out later in the day, but nothing was encountered. Flying Officer Hooper was sent on a base patrol and saw seven Type 97 bombers flying 2000 feet above him. He called for instructions, but there was no reply, so he climbed to attack. As he did so, six Navy 'Zero' fighters dived on to his tail. They swept all over Hooper, easily turning inside him. He rolled his Buffalo onto its back and slid into a power dive for home, eventually escaping his pursuers. Flight Lieutenant 'Kongo' Kinninmont, the B Flight CO, and Sgt Norm Chapman also took off for a reconnaissance sortie over Singora. About two miles from their objective, they were attacked by twelve Ki-27s fighters. They had a hard time against the Japanese, but both eventually made it safely back to base. As soon as they were down, 23 Japanese bombers approached from the north at about 6000 feet, flying lower this time after they had found no real opposition and no anti-aircraft fire put up against the first raiders. At that moment, 21 only had four serviceable Buffaloes. The station commander received orders in the afternoon to withdraw all flyable aircraft to Butterworth airfield and to dispatch his surplus personnel by road in the same direction. However, before that order could be executed, an urgent order came from NORGROUP (whose task it was to control all air units in the Kuala Lumpur area) for a further reconnaissance over Singora. It was F/L Kinninmont who did the job, but he was jumped again, by 'Zeros' this time, on the return flight. Using the same tactics that worked earlier in the day, he managed to return to base, with some bullet holes in his aircraft, to report details of what Japanese activity he saw at Singora. As for the four operational Buffaloes, they departed for Butterworth in the evening (six flyable aircraft had arrived earlier in the day at Butterworth). The squadron, with so few aircraft, could do little from Butterworth so its role was limited to mainly tactical reconnaissance flights.

On the 9th, Flying Officers Geoff Sheppard and Daryl Sproule took off on such a sortie across the Thai border. They had initially been tasked to escort Blenheims, but the bombers stayed on the ground. During the flight, the Buffalo pilots spotted a column of light tanks and enemy motor transport near Jitra that they attacked, leaving four trucks on fire and several others damaged. In the afternoon two more sections of Buffaloes, flown by F/O MacKenny and F/L Williams, and F/O Montefiore and F/L White, took off and circled the aerodrome during an air raid and were engaged by enemy fighters. Dick MacKenny, Williams' wingman, was shot down in flames, but managed to parachute to safety despite suffering facial burns. Williams was not in good position either and decided

The other Australian Buffalo squadron, 21 Sqn, also stationed at Sembawang, lined up after 453 Squadron's aircraft. Above: Sgt G.T. Harrison seated in AN180/GA-B. Behind: Sgt N.R. Chapman in W8224/GA-M. Below: another view of the line-up. In the foreground is Sgt M. Mighall who was a member of the ground crew. He had been asked to wear a Mae West to look like a pilot in order to make up the numbers for the media.

Another view of 21 Sqn on display with Buffalo AN175 at the front.

The retreat from, and evacuation of, Singapore was chaotic and many almost intact Buffaloes fell in to Japanese hands, like AN194/GA-D of 21 Sqn seen here.

to break off and dive for the airfield, but, with the Japanese behind, was forced to make a high speed approach that proved too fast, so he had to go around. The engine coughed and ran out of petrol during the second attempt, but Williams managed to make a successful dead-stick landing. He evacuated his aircraft just before it was strafed and blew up on the runway. The other pair fared no better. Flying Officer Montefiore claimed one opponent shot down, but was then forced to bale out of his stricken aircraft. He landed in a palm tree and managed to get back to Butterworth later in the day. Flight Lieutenant White's Buffalo was also a victim of the Ki-27s and his aircraft was riddled with bullets. He was obliged to make a forced landing on Penang Island. Two days later, AN188 was inspected and found to be extensively damaged and not repairable. Parts were salvaged and the remnants burnt. In the evening, the squadron was ordered to withdraw to Ipoh. Six Buffaloes were still on hand. They arrived at Ipoh on 10 December and S/L Allshorn was asked to reform the squadron. This could be done with twelve replacement Buffaloes. Allshorn departed for Singapore to collect some aircraft, but the number available was less than expected as only six Buffaloes could be found (all from the last batch and may have included AN172, AN179, AN205 and AN206) and all were still in their crates. It would take at least two or three days to unpack and assemble the aircraft. Three Buffaloes from Butterworth were made airworthy the next day and were able to join the others at Ipoh, piloted by volunteers from 62 Squadron who had never flown the type before. By the end of the day, however, mainly due to the armament problems, there were no fully serviceable aircraft available. Allshorn pressed his ground crew to get the replacement Buffaloes airworthy and, eventually, all six were prepared for an early departure on 15 December. However, the weather was far from ideal, with low clouds and rain, and the formation broke up. Allshorn continued on with F/L Kinninmont. The weather continued to worsen so Allshorn decided that it would be unsafe to proceed any further. He chose a short bitumen strip and made a cautious approach, managing to stop without over-running the strip. Kinninmont made three attempts to land. He overran the strip on his fourth attempt and put his aircraft, AN172, on its back. The aircraft was not salvaged. Allshorn received assistance and proceeded by car, leaving his Buffalo to Kinninmont who eventually arrived at Ipoh before dark. The other four pilots elected to return to Singapore individually and all did safely except F/O Hooper who crashed his aircraft in a paddy field, but escaped with only cuts and bruises. They recommenced the journey later in the day, as part of a formation of ten Buffaloes led by S/L Harper of No. 453 Squadron, and this time all reached Ipoh safely. The general situation at Ipoh regarding the Buffaloes was not good, however, especially considering the lack of accommodation, and food was also a major issue. Nevertheless, 21 Squadron, working in conjunction with 453, maintained standing patrols throughout the 16th. This was the only way to tackle raids by the Japanese as the Army had lost its advanced warning outposts. On the negative side, this put extra strain on the pilots, who were in bad shape already, and engine hours were consumed quickly while ground crew struggled valiantly to maintain the aircraft in good condition. The next day, the Japanese sent a raid, but it was 453 that bore the brunt of the attack, with only one of 21 Squadron's pilots getting airborne. Two Buffaloes were destroyed on the ground and a third damaged. Two more raids were made on Ipoh on the 18th,

the bombers waiting until the patrolling Buffaloes had just landed before attacking. Two more Buffaloes were destroyed and three damaged in the attack. The squadron's equipment officer, F/L F.W. Horden was also killed. Also, a non-operational Buffalo of the squadron was also flown to Sembawang with F/O Barry Hood at the controls. That day, Ipoh was once more the victim of an air attack that wrecked F/L Kirkman's aircraft while a second (possibly from 453) was caught in the blast of a bomb and flung on its side with one wing ripped off. It was clear that Ipoh was no longer tenable so the aircraft were ordered to Kuala Lumpur. On arrival at Singapore, 21 and 453 were amalgamated under Harper's command, OC 453 Squadron, while S/L Allshorn was posted to the operations room at Sembawang. Flight Lieutenant W.H. Williams was promoted to squadron leader and took over the squadron, or what remained of it (from this point, the 21 Squadron story continues as part of 453 Squadron's).

As mentioned in the 21/453 part, on 26 January news was received that 21 was to return to Australia. Administrative work began at once and the two squadrons reverted to their previous identities. Sorties were carried out the next day, and on the 28th, although pilot shortages impacted all ops. What had been tasked for 21 comprised a tactical reconnaissance carried out in the middle of the afternoon (F/L Kirkman and F/O Hood). This would be the last operational flight before the gradual return to Australia (with a stop at Palembang in the NEI). Only six pilots remained with 453, including F/L Kinninmont. Embarkation occurred on the 30th with the SS *Takliwa* threatened by a Japanese raid on the dock and harbour. Fortunately, no damage was reported by the ship. The voyage was uneventful and the squadron disembarked at Palembang on 1 February 1942. As a far as the Buffalo was concerned, its association with 21 Squadron was over, the unit being repatriated two weeks later.

Claims - 21 Squadron RAAF (Confirmed and Probable)

Date	Pilot	SN	Origin	Type	Serial	Code	Nb	Cat.
09.12.41	F/O Harold V. **Montefiore**	Aus. 290629	RAAF	Ki-27	**W8236**		1.0	C

Total: 1.0

Summary of the aircraft lost on Operations - 21 Squadron RAAF

Date	Pilot	S/N	Origin	Serial	Code	Fate
09.12.41	F/O Clifford R. **McKenny**	Aus. 574	RAAF	**W8224**		-
	F/L Fredrick H. **Williams**	Aus. 479	RAAF	**W8232**		-
	F/O Harold V. **Montefiore**	Aus. 290629	RAAF	**W8236**		-
	F/O Alan M. **White**	Aus. 573	RAAF	**AN188**		-
14.12.41	F/O Alan M. **White**	Aus. 573	RAAF	**AN201**		†

Total: 5

Entering combat on 8 December 1941, only eight Buffaloes were still part of the RAF inventory three months later. If the eighteen Buffaloes wrecked before the Japanese invasion are deducted, more than 150 aircraft were destroyed or abandoned in that period of time. However, it must be added that the air raids were responsible for the destruction of at least thirty, 21 in Malaya and nine in Burma. Many more, around forty, damaged to varying degrees, could not be repaired and were either used for spares or abandoned. In the end, only 55 or so Buffaloes were lost to direct enemy action while more than twenty were lost to non-operational incidents. Against those losses, an estimate of 116 claims for confirmed or probably destroyed aircraft can be ascertained despite the destruction of many documents during the evacuation of Singapore and Burma making it difficult to deduce anything more than approximate calculations. Therefore the ratio is not as bad as is often reported. The Hawker Hurricane in the region didn't do any better and the Finns with their 44 B-239s (with the less powerful engine) claimed close to 500 victories against Soviet aircraft. While the Buffalo was inferior to the Hurricane and the Spitfire, to deploy the latter in the Far East would not have avoided the disaster from the RAF's perspective, but there possibly would have been more claims made. The RAF in the region had to rely on young pilots, freshly graduated from training, facing very experienced Japanese pilots who had been fighting in China for many years and who were equipped with the finest performing fighters of the time. In those conditions, even the introduction of the Spitfire would have had little impact on the issue.

The RAAF took charge of some Brewster B339-23s from the Dutch and these received the Australian denomination 'A51'. A51-13, was returned to the Fifth AF in July 1943 and was scrapped soon after.

At Singapore, the RAAF was issued with Buffaloes from the RAF order (B-339E). The RAAF also used the Buffalo in Australia, but those aircraft were from the Dutch order. The Dutch had showed great interest in the Brewster fighter and two models were eventually produced (B-339C and B-339D) to serve in the military aviation arm in the Netherlands East Indies, the ML-KNIL. The order of 71 B-339C/D had been delivered by September 1941, but, early in the year, the Netherlands Purchasing Commission in the USA was continuing to seek additional Brewster fighters (the 72nd aircraft was kept in the US for repairs). While there was no problem for Brewster to deliver the new order, the engine manufacturers were facing considerable delays in producing new engines. Consequently, due to the shortage of the particular Cyclone model powering the B-339C/D models, the Dutch had to accept the installation of the 950hp Wright R-1820-G5 for the twenty B-339s purchased in the second order. This model was the B-339-23 and was identical to the B-339D in all respects but the forward fuselage as, like the F2A-3, that was extended by ten inches. This model, from the start, was underpowered, but the Dutch had no alternative. When Java surrendered in March 1942, the four ships carrying the twenty aircraft, and the last B-339D, were still at sea so they were diverted to Australia, arriving between 9 March and 9 April 1942. They were slowly assembled and initially assigned to the US Fifth Air Force in Australia. As the Americans had no need for such a fighter, they released seventeen of them to a RAAF in desperate need of modern aircraft. All were B-339-23 models. They received the serials A51-1 to A51-17. The aircraft that survived RAAF use were returned to the USAAF during the summer of 1943.

No. 24 Squadron RAAF
This unit used a handful of Buffaloes in the summer of 1943, all allotted from No. 85 Squadron. The first to be issued was A51-3 on 11 June. It was followed two weeks later by A51-10, 11, 12 and 14 while A51-3 then departed. This unit was earmarked to serve in

New Guinea with Vultee Vengeances. Little flying was done on Buffaloes before the squadron left for its operational deployment in September 1943.

No. 25 Squadron RAAF

Until the war, 25 Squadron, a militia unit based at Pearce, near Perth, Western Australia, was mostly engaged in Army support tasks, naval co-operation work, meteorological flying and pilot cadet training. After September, the equipment was standardised on the CAC Wirraway and its role was limited to anti-submarine patrols and convoy escorts. In March 1942, with Australia facing a possible invasion from Japan, the role of 25 was changed. The Perth area had to be reinforced, particularly air defence. During the summer it was decided to allocate Buffaloes as an interim measure, P-39 Airacobras being the intended fighter type, but these never materialised. Some fighter pilots with experience on the type were posted in. Flight Lieutenant H.V. Montifiore, formerly of 21 Squadron in Singapore earlier in the year, arrived in the first week of August. The first Buffalo arrived on the 14th, soon to be repaired after suffering a landing accident. It was aircraft No. 302 (later A51-8). The next day, other Buffaloes were taken on charge – Aircraft 301 (A51-7), 305 (A51-9), 307 (A51-10), 380 (A51-11), 309 (A51-12), 310 (A51-13), 311 (A51-14), and 312 (A51-15) – but all were operationally unserviceable due to a lack of armament. Buffalo strength was to be six operational aircraft, with three being held in reserve, to form C Flight. The squadron was also using seventeen Wirraways. The career of the Buffaloes with the unit was uneventful, ignoring some minor accidents, the most serious incident being when A51-8, piloted by S/L W.H. Williams, the OC and formerly CO of 21 Squadron at Singapore, collided with a bird while flying in the vicinity of Dunreath (where the main Perth airport is). He managed to make a safe landing with a large dent in the leading edge of the starboard wing. The aircraft was repaired and returned to service. Very few operational flights were recorded. On 4 January 1943, a fighter escort and a reconnaissance patrol were flown over the SS *Chungking* sailing off the coast. The one hour 45 minute flight was carried out by three Buffaloes (A51-10, 11 and 13) and was led by the CO. This op was repeated the next day by A51-10, 11, 13, 15, again led by the CO. On 2 February, Sgt R.A.E. Taylor ground-looped A51-15 during take-off, but without major consequence. That was the last event of note before C Flight was moved to No. 85 Squadron on formation at Guildford.

No. 85 Squadron RAAF

This squadron was formed on 12 February 1943 at Guildford, and the nucleus was provided by C Flight of 25 Squadron with its nine Buffaloes. The new CO was also from 25 Squadron, S/L C.N. Daly. The squadron was to be based at Dunreath aerodrome. Formation hampered the squadron's flying activities in February, but flights started in March and about ninety of all kinds were performed, with about 115 the following month. However, April also saw the arrival of the first CAC Boomerang. Consequently, the number of Buffalo flights decreased in May, to about a dozen, the last operational Brewster fighter being A51-14. A last test flight was carried on A51-11 on 7 May.

No. 1 Photographic Reconnaissance Unit RAAF

The first and main unit to be equipped with the Buffalo in Australia was No. 1 Photographic Reconnaissance Unit (PRU) formed on 8 June 1942 at Laverton, Victoria. The immediate intention was for the Buffaloes to be converted for the photo reconnaissance task by removing all armour plating and armament, and installing auxiliary petrol tanks and three F24 cameras. The mission of the unit was to carry out long-range strategic and tactical reconnaissance in the form of high altitude photography using a camera fitted with a long focal length lens. Command was given to S/L L.W. Law. By the end of the month, Buffaloes A51-1, 2, 3, 5 and 6 had been

Line up of Brewster 339-23 of 25 Squadron RAAF at Pierce in 1942 with A51-11 and A51-10 in the forfront. Those two were returned to the USAAF in 1943. Note teh third B-339 with the old RAF style roundeL. *(AHM of WA)*

taken on charge and training was underway. Operations could not be flown as none of the Buffaloes had yet been modified. Buffalo A51-4, which was also issued, never arrived at the unit as it fell victim to an accident on 16 June and was converted to components. In July, the first dramatic event occurred when F/L R.H. Winter was killed in the crash of A51-2 three miles south of Tallarook and 1.5 miles east of the Hume Highway. In August, the unit moved to Hughes Field in the north-western area, but the complete move, initiated on the 12th, was only completed on 9 September. On 23 August 1942, the airfield suffered a Japanese raid that destroyed one Buffalo (A51-6) and the unit's Wirraway (A20-599). It was at Hughes Field that the modifications to the Buffaloes were carried out. At Hughes, training intensified with the three remaining aircraft (A51-1, 3 and 5). During a training flight, Sgt J. Austin, who had fought in Singapore with 21 Squadron, was killed when he crashed A51-5 at Derby on 25 September. At the beginning of October, all unit pilots were ready to commence operations when suitable aircraft were made available. Actually, by 30 September, only A51-1 was serviceable as A51-3 was waiting for spares. In October, although handicapped by having just one aircraft on hand, and unsuitable weather conditions for clear photography work, some demands by the Army, Area RAAF HQ, camouflage section and AA units, could be fulfilled. However, towards the end of the month, four officers were sent back to Laverton to complete their photographic training and be converted to the P-43 Lancer (see Squadrons! 9) while two Lockheed F-4 reconnaissance aircraft arrived at the squadron (see Squadrons! 9). As for Buffaloes, A51-1 was kept in flying condition by removing parts from A51-3. It flew close to sixty hours in October. While another move to Coomalie Creek was under preparation, training continued on the Buffalo, three new pilots being converted, but from the 15th onwards A51-1 was unserviceable with undercarriage trouble and a necessary 240 hours inspection. The time flown by A51-1 in November dropped to 35.1 hours. The aircraft was sent to Amberley for its inspection. Eventually, both Buffaloes returned to airworthy condition in January, A51-1 returning from Amberley and A51-3, so far stuck at Hughes, made its way to Coomalie Creek. That month, A51-1 made four local reconnaissance flights on the 14th, 20th, 24th and 26th. The situation remained unchanged in February and the Buffaloes flew 34.3 hours. Six photography flights were performed including four flown by the CO on the 24th. In March, 36.7 hours were flown by the two Buffaloes and sixteen photography flights were carried out. It must be said that the Buffalo was the type most used in March. The same applied to April with 67.1 hours flown and 36 photography flights. In May, A51-1 left the unit for an engine change. Despite that, 44.4 hours were flown for the month. In June, the last Brewster eventually left the unit, being allocated to No. 24 Squadron, a temporary measure as the aircraft was due to be returned to the Americans. This aircraft flew 20.9 hours in June for 1 PRU.

Date	Pilot	S/N	Origin	Serial	Code	Fate
08.07.42	F/L Raymond H. **Winter**	Aus. 648	RAAF	**A51-2**		†
25.09.42	Sgt James **Austin**	Aus. 404699	RAAF	**A51-5**		†
		Total: 2				

✝

IN MEMORIAM
Brewster Buffalo

Name	Service No	Rank	Age	Origin	Date	Serial
ARTHUR, Vincent	NZ405519	Sgt	19	RNZAF	22.01.42	W8147
AUSTIN, James	AUS. 404699	Sgt	24	RAAF	25.09.42	A51-5
BALDWIN, Mervyn John Fitzhardinge	RAF No. 771896	Sgt	33	RAF	22.01.42	W8187
BREWER, Paul Middleton	NZ402565	P/O	22	RNZAF	20.01.42	W8229
BROWN, David Roderick Llewelyn	NZ41867	P/O	24	RNZAF	13.12.41	W8158
CHAPMAN, Norman Richard	AUS. 401102	Sgt	26	RAAF	18.01.42	AN174
CHARTERS, Cecil Deryk*	NZ41876	W/O	29	RNZAF	25.12.43	AN189
COX, Renest Wilkin	NZ41881	P/O	22	RNZAF	18.01.42	W8141
CRAIG, Alexander Gray	NZ41882	Sgt	23	RNZAF	18.12.41	W8175
DRURY, Robert William	AUS. 207698	P/O	24	RAAF	22.12.41	AN204
ELLIOTT, Paul Lester	NZ402467	Sgt	19	RNZAF	05.01.42	W8199
FARR, Leonard Raymond	NZ411390	P/O	24	RNZAF	25.01.42	W8191
FINN, John Gilbert	NZ404859	Sgt	22	RNZAF	20.01.42	W8240
HESKETH, Greville Lloyd	NZ402868	P/O	26	RNZAF	15.01.42	W8183
HEWITT, Edward Bertram	NZ405269	Sgt	19	RNZAF	25.12.41	W8248
IRVINE-BROWN, Maxwell	AUS. 404736	P/O	20	RAAF	18.10.41	W8208
LAMBERT, John Edward	RAF No. 40924	F/L	23	RAF	25.12.41	W8220
MACPHERSON, John	NZ41486	Sgt	25	RNZAF	25.12.41	AN216
McANENY, Kenneth Jack	NZ411421	P/O	19	RNZAF	18.01.42	W8171
McNABB, Ronald Percy	NZ404393	Sgt	19	RNZAF	25.12.41	W8206
NEWMAN, Reginald James	NZ41995	Sgt	22	RNZAF	12.01.42	W8137
NEAL, Leonard James	RAF No. 29174	W/C	37	RAF	13.12.41	W8176
OELRICH, Ronald Reginald	AUS. 402875	Sgt	23	RAAF	13.12.41	W8225
OLIVER, John Benjamin	NZ402888	Sgt	23	RNZAF	15.01.42	W8178
PARSONS, Henry Wrefrod	AUS. 407802	Sgt	23	RAAF	19.01.42	AN170
PETERSON, Eric Anton	AUS. 402951	Sgt	24	RAAF	22.12.41	W8207
PINCKNEY, David John Colin	RAF No. 72520	F/L	24	RAF	23.01.42	W8239
RANKIN, Noel Bain	NZ404942	Sgt	28	RNZAF	12.01.42	W8234
READ, Malcolm Neville	AUS. 402952	Sgt	24	RAAF	22.12.41	AN175
REYNOLDS, Arthur Russell	NZ405819	Sgt	19	RNZAF	13.01.42	W8238
SHIELD, Ronald Spencer	NZ404954	P/O	23	RNZAF	05.01.42	W8179
WHITE, Alan Maxwell	AUS. 573	F/L	25	RAAF	14.12.41	AN201
WIGGLESWORTH, John Spencer	RAF No. 42930	F/O	21	RAF	06.02.42	W8213
WINTER, Raymond Henry	AUS. 648	F/L	28	RAAF	08.07.42	A51-2

Total: 34
Australia: 10, New Zealand: 19, UK: 5

*As a PoW

The wreckage of W8137/WP-C of 243. It crashed on 12 January 1942 killing the pilot Sgt R.J. Newman. *(C.T. Kronk via P. Sortehaug)*

Brewster Buffalo Mk. I W8245
No. 67 Squadron
Mingaladon (Burma), December 1941

Brewster Buffalo Mk. I W8147
No. 243 Squadron
Sergeant Geoffrey B. FISKEN (RNZAF)
Kallang (Singapore), December 1941

Brewtser Buffalo Mk. I W8205
No. 453 (RAAF) Squadron
Sembawang (Singapore), December 1941

Brewtser Buffalo Mk. I W8231
No. 453 (RAAF) Squadron
Sembawang (Singapore), December 1941

Brewster Buffalo Mk. I W8138
No. 488 (NZ) Squadron
Pilot Officer Noel C. SHARP (RNZAF)
Kallang (Singapore), December 1941

Brewtser Buffalo Mk. I W8236
No. 21 (RAAF) Squadron
Sembawang (Singapore), December 1941

SQUADRONS! - The series

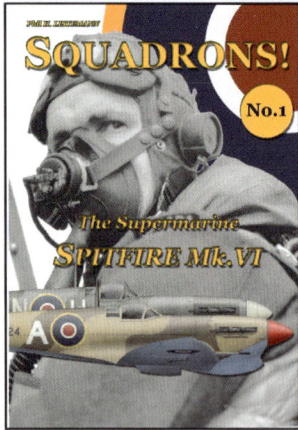

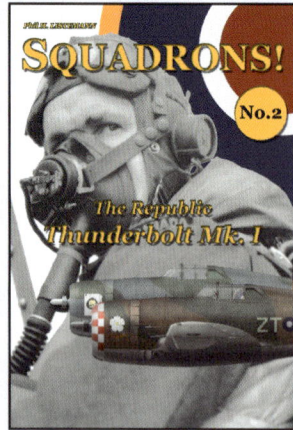

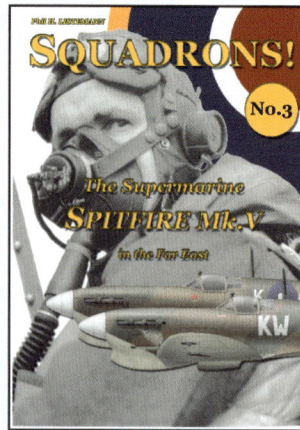

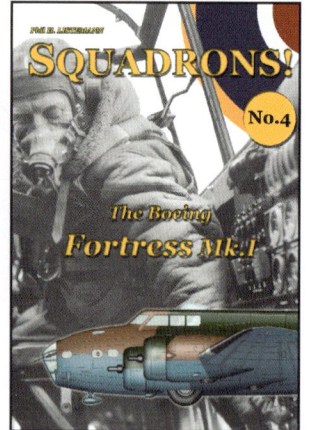

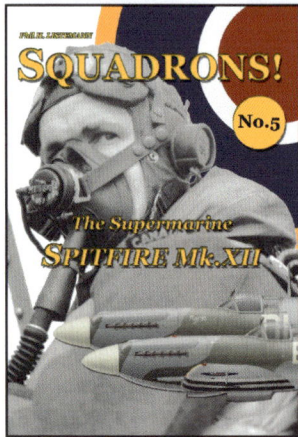

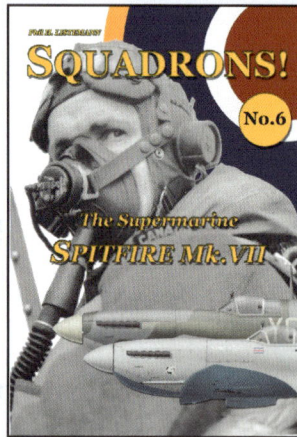

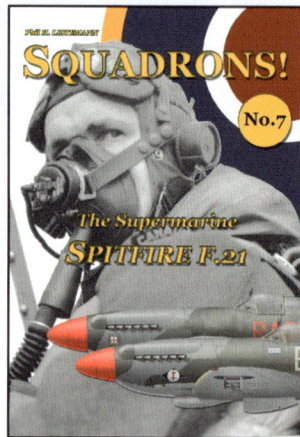

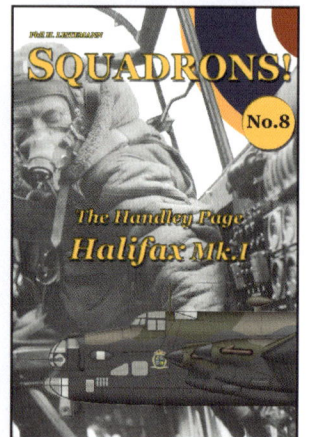

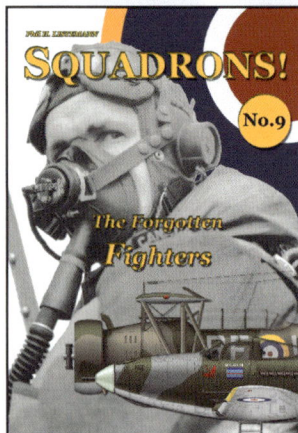

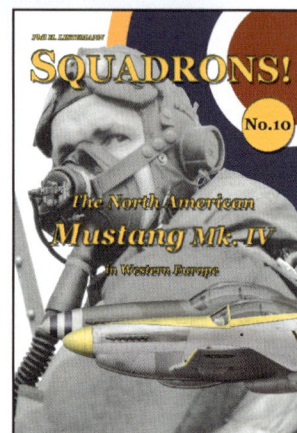

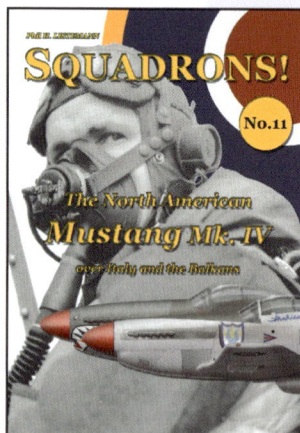

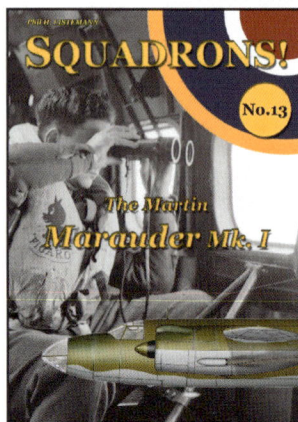

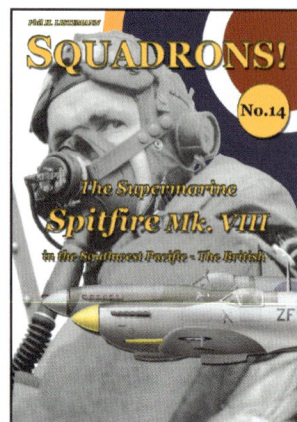

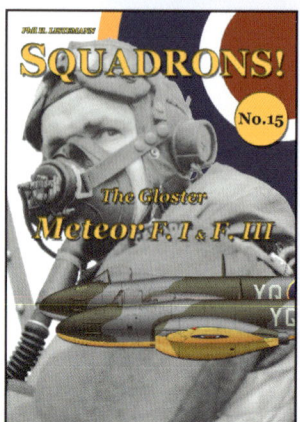

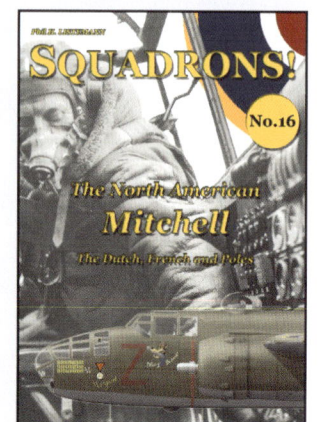

No.1 — Phil H. Listemann — SQUADRONS! — *The Supermarine* **SPITFIRE Mk.VI**

No.2 — Phil H. Listemann — SQUADRONS! — *The Republic* **Thunderbolt Mk. I**

No.3 — Phil H. Listemann — SQUADRONS! — *The Supermarine* **SPITFIRE Mk.V** *in the Far East*

No.4 — Phil H. Listemann — SQUADRONS! — *The Boeing* **Fortress Mk.I**

No.5 — Phil H. Listemann — SQUADRONS! — *The Supermarine* **SPITFIRE Mk.XII**

No.6 — Phil H. Listemann — SQUADRONS! — *The Supermarine* **SPITFIRE Mk.VII**

No.7 — Phil H. Listemann — SQUADRONS! — *The Supermarine* **SPITFIRE F.21**

No.8 — Phil H. Listemann — SQUADRONS! — *The Handley Page* **Halifax Mk.I**

No.9 — Phil H. Listemann — SQUADRONS! — *The Forgotten* **Fighters**

No.10 — Phil H. Listemann — SQUADRONS! — *The North American* **Mustang Mk. IV** *in Western Europe*

No.11 — Phil H. Listemann — SQUADRONS! — *The North American* **Mustang Mk. IV** *over Italy and the Balkans*

No.12 — Phil H. Listemann — SQUADRONS! — *The Supermarine* **Spitfire Mk. XVI** *- The British -*

No.13 — Phil H. Listemann — SQUADRONS! — *The Martin* **Marauder Mk. I**

No.14 — Phil H. Listemann — SQUADRONS! — *The Supermarine* **Spitfire Mk. VIII** *in the Southwest Pacific - The British*

No.15 — Phil H. Listemann — SQUADRONS! — *The Gloster* **Meteor F.1 s F. III**

No.16 — Phil H. Listemann — SQUADRONS! — *The North American* **Mitchell** *The Dutch, French and Poles*

SQUADRONS! No.17 — The Curtiss *Mohawk*

SQUADRONS! No.18 — The Curtiss *Kittyhawk Mk II*

SQUADRONS! No.19 — The Boulton Paul *Defiant* - Day and Night fighter

SQUADRONS! No.20 — The Supermarine *Spitfire Mk. VIII* - in the Southwest Pacific - The Australians

SQUADRONS! No.21 — The Boeing *Fortress Mk. II & Mk. III*

SQUADRONS! No.22 — The Douglas *Boston & Havoc* - The Australians

SQUADRONS! No.23 — The Republic *Thunderbolt Mk. II*

SQUADRONS! No.24 — The Douglas *Boston & Havoc* - Night Fighter

SQUADRONS! No.25 — The Supermarine *SPITFIRE Mk.V* - The Eagle Squadrons

SQUADRONS! No.26 — The Hawker *Hurricane Mk. I & II* - The Canadians

SQUADRONS! No.27 — The Supermarine *SPITFIRE Mk.V* - The Bombing Squadrons

SQUADRONS! No.28 — The Consolidated B-24 *Liberator* - The Australians

SQUADRONS! No.29 — The Supermarine *Spitfire Mk. XVI* - The Dominions

SQUADRONS! No.30 — The Supermarine *SPITFIRE Mk.V* - The Belgian & Dutch Squadrons

SQUADRONS! No.31 — The Supermarine *SPITFIRE Mk.V* - The New-Zealanders

SQUADRONS! No.32 — The Supermarine *SPITFIRE Mk.V* - The Norwegians

Phil H. Listemann

Printed in Great Britain
by Amazon